THE REALM OF TRUTH

Ille potens sui
laetusque deget cui licet in diem
dixisse, vixi. Cras vel atra
nube polum Pater occupato
vel sole puro : non tamen irritum
quodcumque retro est efficiet, neque
diffinget infectumque reddet
quod fugiens semel hora vexit.

HORACE.

Whatever withdraws us from the power of the
senses, whatever makes the past the distant, or the
future predominate over the present, advances us in
the dignity of thinking beings.

DR. JOHNSON.

It fortifies my soul to know
That, though I wander, Truth is so.

CLOUGH.

THE
REALM OF TRUTH

BOOK THIRD
OF
REALMS OF BEING

BY

GEORGE SANTAYANA

NEW YORK
CHARLES SCRIBNER'S SONS
1938

COPYRIGHT, 1937, 1938, BY
GEORGE SANTAYANA

———

Printed in the United States of America

PREFACE

An unsophisticated reader will find no difficulty in understanding the sense in which the word truth is used in this book. It is the sense which the word bears in ordinary conversation; and such refinements as I may be led to suggest are not calculated to subvert the plain signification of the word, but only to clarify and confirm it. In this matter, as in many others, I follow common sense; not indeed in its conventions, not in respect to popular dogmas which may be local, verbal, mythical, and contradictory; but I follow common sense in its general momentum and presuppositions, which are indeed the only possible foundation of science, of literature, and of human intercourse.

Nevertheless, it is the business of philosophers, in using the categories of common sense—as they must if they are to be consistent and intelligible—incidentally to criticize and to reform them. The category of truth in particular has been lately subjected to rough usage: and those who live in the thick of contemporary controversies, particularly in America, may well ask me, with a certain irritation, what on earth I can mean by *truth*. In deference to these experts in logic, let me begin by explaining how I use that word. In fact, I have explained it already on sundry occasions; and I can hardly do better than collect here a few of those incidental explanations. They will pave the way innocently and conveniently to the discussions that are to follow.

v

The truth properly means the sum of all true propositions, what omniscience would assert, the whole ideal system of qualities and relations which the world has exemplified or will exemplify. The truth is all things seen under the form of eternity. . . . Every thinking man always assumes the reality of an actual truth, comprehensive and largely undiscovered, of which he claims to be reporting a portion. What (the psychological critic) rather confusingly calls truth, and wishes to reduce to a pragmatic function, is not this underlying truth, the sum of all true propositions, but merely the abstract quality which all true propositions must have in common, to be called true. By truth he means only correctness. The possibility of correctness in an idea is a great puzzle to him, on account of his idealism, which identifies ideas with their objects; and he asks himself how an idea can ever come to be correct or incorrect, as if it referred to something beyond itself.

The fact is, of course, that an idea can be correct or incorrect only if by the word idea we mean not a datum but an opinion; and the abstract relation of correctness, by virtue of which any opinion is true, is easily stated. An opinion is true if what it is talking about is constituted as the opinion asserts it to be constituted. . . . It is not a question of similarity or derivation between a passive datum and a hidden object; it is a question of identity between a fact asserted and a fact existing. If an opinion could not freely leap to its object, no matter how distant or hypothetical, and assert something of that chosen object, an opinion could not be so much as wrong; for it would not be an opinion about anything.[1]

The experience which perhaps makes even the empiricist awake to the being of truth, and brings it home to any energetic man, is the experience of other people lying. When I am falsely accused, or when I am represented as thinking what I do not think, I rebel against that contradiction to my evident self-knowledge; and as the other man asserts that the liar is myself, and a third person might very well entertain that

[1] *Character and Opinion in the United States* (London, Constable & Company, Ltd., 1920), pp. 153-6.

hypothesis and decide against me, I learn that a report may fly in the face of the facts. There is, I then see clearly, a comprehensive standard description for every fact, which those who report it as it happened repeat in part, whereas on the contrary liars contradict it in some particular. And a little further reflection may convince me that even the liar must recognize the fact to some extent, else it would not be *that* fact that he was misrepresenting; and also that honest memory and belief, even when most unimpeachable, are not exhaustive and not themselves the standard for belief or for memory, since they are now clearer and now vaguer, and subject to error and correction. That standard comprehensive description of any fact which neither I nor any man can ever wholly repeat, is the truth about it.[1]

When "truth" is used in the abstract sense of correctness, or the quality which all correct judgments have in common, another word, perhaps "fact" or "reality", would . . . have to be used for that standard comprehensive description of the object to which correct judgments conform. But a fact is not a description of itself; and as to the word "reality", if it is understood to mean existence, it too cannot designate a description, which is an essence only. Facts are transitory: . . . and when they have lapsed, it is only their essence that subsists and that, being partially recovered and assigned to them in a retrospective judgment, can render this judgment true. Opinions are true or false by repeating or contradicting some part of the truth about the facts which they envisage; and this truth about the facts is the standard comprehensive description of them.[2]

Truth is not an opinion, even an ideally true one; because besides the limitation in scope which human opinions, at least, can never escape, even the most complete and accurate opinion would give precedence to some terms, and have a direction of survey; and this direction might be changed or reversed without lapsing into error; so that the truth is the

---

[1] *Scepticism and Animal Faith* (London, Constable & Company, Ltd., 1923), p. 266.
[2] Ibid., p. 267.

field which various true opinions traverse in various directions, and no opinion itself. An even more impressive difference between truth and any true discourse is that discourse is an event; it has a date not that of its subject-matter, even if the subject-matter be existential, and roughly contemporary; and in human beings discourse is conversant almost entirely with the past only, whereas truth is dateless and absolutely identical whether the opinions which seek to reproduce it arise before or after the event which the truth describes.[1]

If there were no absolute truth, all-inclusive and eternal, the desultory views taken from time to time by individuals would themselves be absolute. They would be irrelevant to one another, and incomparable in point of truth, each being without any object but the essence which appeared in it. If views can be more or less correct, and perhaps complementary to one another, it is because they refer to the same system of nature, the complete description of which, covering the whole past and the whole future, would be the absolute truth. This absolute truth is . . . that segment of the realm of essence which happens to be illustrated in existence. The question whether a given essence belongs to this segment or not—that is, whether a suggested idea is or is not true—has a tragic importance for an animal intent on discovering and describing what exists, or has existed, or is destined to exist in his world. He seldom has leisure to dwell on essences apart from their presumable truth; even their beauty and dialectical pattern seem to him rather trivial unless they are significant of facts in the realm of matter, controlling his destiny. I therefore give a special name to this tragic segment of the realm of essence and call it the *Realm of Truth*.[2]

A comprehensive description (of any fact) includes also all the radiations of that fact—I mean, all that perspective of the world of facts and of the realm of essence which is obtained by taking this fact as a centre and viewing everything else only in relation with it. The truth about any fact is therefore infinitely extended, although it grows thinner, so

[1] *Scepticism and Animal Faith.*, p. 268.
[2] *The Realm of Essence* (London, Constable & Company, Ltd., 1928), Preface to Realms of Being, p. xv.

to speak, as you travel from it to further and further facts, or to less and less relevant ideas. It is the splash any fact makes, or the penumbra it spreads, by dropping through the realm of essence. Evidently no opinion can embrace it all, or identify itself with it; nor can it be identified with the facts to which it relates, since they are in flux, and it is eternal.[1]

The eternity of truth is inherent in it: all truths—not a few grand ones—are equally eternal. . . . Inspired people, who are too hot to think, often identify the truth with their own tenets. . . . Eternal truths . . . are then tenets which the remotest ancestors of man are reputed to have held, and which his remotest descendants are forbidden to abandon. Of course there are no eternal tenets: neither the opinions of men, nor mankind, nor anything existent can be eternal; eternity is a property of essences only. Even if all the spirits in heaven and earth had been so far unanimous on any point of doctrine, there is no reason, except the monotony and inertia of nature, why their logic or religion or morals should not change to-morrow from top to bottom, if they all suddenly grew wiser or differently foolish.[2]

The truth, however nobly it may loom before the scientific intellect, is ontologically something secondary. Its eternity is but the wake of the ship of time, a furrow which matter must plough upon the face of essence. Truth must have a subject-matter, it must be the truth about something: and it is the character of this moving object, lending truth and definition to the truth itself, that is substantial and fundamental in the universe.[3]

The tide of evolution carries everything before it, thoughts no less than bodies, and persons no less than nations. Yet all things are eternal in their status, as truth is. The place which an event fills in history is its inalienable place; the character that an act or a feeling possesses in passing is its inalienable character. Now the human mind is not merely animal, not merely absorbed in the felt transition from one

[1] *Scepticism and Animal Faith*, pp. 267–8.
[2] Ibid., pp. 268–9.   [3] Ibid., pp. 227–8.

state of life to another. It is partly synthetic, intellectual, contemplative, able to look before and after and to see fleeting things at once in their mutual relations, or, as Spinoza expressed it, under the form of eternity. To see things under the form of eternity is to see them in their historic and moral truth, not as they seemed as they passed, but as they remain when they are over. When a man's life is over, it remains true that he has lived; it remains true that he has been one sort of man and not another. In the infinite mosaic of history that bit has its unfading colour and its perpetual function and effect. A man who understands himself under the form of eternity knows the quality that eternally belongs to him, and knows that he cannot wholly die, even if he would; for when the movement of his life is over, the truth of his life remains. The fact of him is a part for ever of the infinite context of facts. . . . The animals are mortal without knowing it, and doubtless presume, in their folly, that they will live for ever. Man alone knows that he must die; but that very knowledge raises him, in a sense, above mortality, by making him a sharer in the vision of eternal truth. He becomes the spectator of his own tragedy; he sympathizes so much with the fury of the storm that he has no ears left for the shipwrecked sailor, though the sailor were his own soul. The truth is cruel, but it can be loved, and it makes free those who have loved it.[1]

To those who can conceive and love the truth in that sense, this book is addressed.

[1] Introduction to *Spinoza's Ethics* in Everyman's Library (London, J. M. Dent & Sons, 1910), pp. xviii and xix.

CONTENTS

xi

CONTENTS

CONTENTS

CHAPTER I

THERE ARE NO NECESSARY TRUTHS

TRADITION is rich in maxims called necessary truths, such as that $2 + 2 = 4$, that space and time are infinitely divisible, that everything has a cause, and that God, or the most real of beings, necessarily exists. Many such propositions may be necessary, by virtue of the definitions given to their terms; many may be true, in that the facts of nature confirm them; and some may be both necessary logically and true materially, but even then the necessity will come from one quarter and the truth from another.

Logical necessity connects ideal terms.

This conclusion would be evident to anyone who had clearly conceived the nature of infinite Being or the realm of essence; a conception in itself easy and inevitable, when once attention has lighted upon it. So obvious and easy is this conception that it may be regarded as trivial and not worth dwelling on: yet here it finds a momentous echo, which dispels half the doubts and worries of speculation. For if essences, or possible terms of thought, are infinite in number and variety, it follows that every particular fact is contingent, arbitrary, and logically unnecessary, since infinite alternatives were open to existence, if existence had chosen to take a different form. Now it is precisely this unnecessary, arbitrary, contingent chance or fatality, making existence at each point such as it is, that determines what shall be true: that is, what elements of essence shall

But truth, being a radiation of existence, is contingent.

I

figure in that existence. So that, truth being descriptive of existence and existence being contingent, truth will be contingent also.

Let me analyse, on these principles, the four maxims adduced above.

That $2 + 2 = 4$, like all the rest of mathematics, is an equation making explicit certain essential relations between certain terms. Essential relations are all necessary, being based on the definitions or intuitions which distinguish those related terms; though it is by no means necessary or even possible to explore and make explicit in human discourse all the essential relations of the terms selected.[1] Naturally in human mathematics there is a human element. Each intuitive mind darts in its own congenial direction, and sees what a differently intuitive mind might have overlooked: and the range of thought also is human, like its pace and direction. One mind crawls where another wears seven-league boots; yet by whatever leaps or on whatever scale the survey be made, if the essences first chosen are not dropped and confused with others, all explorations will help to fill in the same map, and the science of essence, in that region, will be enriched and consolidated.

Mathematical equations cogent formally.

So far truth has not been broached and mathematics is like music, freely exploring the possibilities of form. And yet, notoriously, mathematics holds true of things; hugs and permeates them far more closely than does confused and inconstant human perception; so that the dream of many exasperated critics of human error has been to assimilate all science to mathematics,

Their applicability a matter of fact.

---

[1] The question does not arise whether mathematical judgments are analytic or synthetic. Psychologically all judgments and all intuitions of the complex are synthetic, because the terms given are distinguished and compared in thought. But if the judgments are necessary, they must be analytical logically, i.e. founded on the nature of the terms.

so as to make knowledge safe by making it, as Locke wished, direct perception of the relations between ideas. Unfortunately, knowledge would then never touch those matters of fact on which Locke was intent. The only serious value of those logical explorations would lie in their possible relevance to the accidents of existence. It is only in that relation and in that measure that mathematical science would cease to be mere play with ideas and would become *true*: that is, in a serious sense, would become *knowledge*. Now the seriousness of mathematics comes precisely of its remarkable and exact relevance to material facts, both familiar and remote: so that mathematical equations, besides being essentially necessary in themselves, are often also true of the world we live in. And this in a surprising measure. For when once any essence falls within the sphere of truth, all its essential relations do so too: and the necessity of these relations will, on that hypothesis, form a necessary complement to a proposition that happens to be true. This same necessity, however, would have nothing to do with truth if the terms it connects were not exemplified in existence.

In this way mathematical calculations far outrunning experiment often turn out to be true of the physical world, as if, *per impossibile*, they could be true *à priori*. But in fact nature, that had to have some form or other, is organized and deployed on principles which, in human language, are called number, shape, and measurable time; categories *They are actually true of the material sphere, at least in the gross.* which for that reason have taken root in human language and science. Yet these categories would have no truth or applicability whatever, if existence were entirely mental and sentimental. They would then be ideal fictions or games of apperception, with their own sporting rules, like the game of chess, but with no

4 THE REALM OF TRUTH

cognitive function in respect to the dynamic world
in which life would arise, and in which these games
would be carried on.

Now as a matter of fact there is a psychological
sphere to which logic and mathematics do not apply.
There, the truth is dramatic. That $2+2=4$ is
not true of ideas. One idea added to another,
in actual intuition, makes still only one idea,
or it makes three: for the combination, with
the relations perceived, forms one complex essence,
and yet the original essences remain distinct, as elements in this new whole. This holds of all moral,
æsthetic, and historical units: they are merged and
reconstituted with every act of apperception. Each
essence evoked reverts, when lost sight of, to its limbo
of latent forms. It cannot contribute genetically or
dynamically, being unsubstantial, to compose the next
apparition. Although life in plants and animals may
be capable of mathematical treatment at one pervasive
material level, none of the vital unities or tropes are
so capable. Moreover, this is not due altogether to
the imagination superposing its views on the flux of
existence: for the special organic unity which breeds
imagination and will, and superposes them on events,
cannot be itself imaginary, since it creates a specific
fact—namely, this very will or imagination. There
are therefore levels of reality, and these the most
important to mankind, that elude all mathematical
axioms.

In the second maxim adduced, that space and time
are infinitely divisible, we pass to an axiom the truth
of which is extremely doubtful, even in the
physical world. Specious space and time
(that is, extension and duration as given to
intuition, and space and time as defined
geometrically) are indeed infinitely divisible. Scale
in them is elastic and utterly unsubstantial, so that

*But irre-
levant to the
realm of
spirit.*

*Physical
space and
time not
subject to
dialectic.*

there is room for the most elaborate ideal event or object within the smallest fraction of time or space. But this hardly seems to be true in the chemical or animal or astronomical spheres, where scale is not variable fantastically: and this for the best of reasons—namely, that in nature empty space and time do not pre-exist, so that existent beings of extensible and unascertainable dimensions may drop into them later; but on the contrary a physical flux, pulsing through natural moments and carrying a definite volume of events with it, creates a real time by its rhythms and a real space by its organic complexity. These native dimensions of the real may indeed be measured and graphically noted in our science, as living music may be measured and noted in a musical score: but the ideal qualities of the medium for such a transcription can no more be imposed on nature by our definitions than the flatness or infinite divisibility of the paper, or the lines of the clef, can impose their graphic qualities upon music.

For want of making this distinction, hopeless difficulties and fatuous assertions have been imported into philosophy. Sometimes nature has been abolished for not conforming to logic: and sometimes logic has corrected nature so as to secure an agreement. Yet the *true* agreement existed from the first, within its natural limits: a friendly concomitance between material events and the free symbolism proper to animal sense or imagination, excited as these must be by those material contacts and organic tensions. There is both precision and poetry in the intricacies of essence, if selectively explored: but the scientific imagination is idolatrous when it interpolates its creations in the dynamic structure of nature. They describe that structure from without, they are not contained within it: they are transcripts, not insights.

When we pass to the third maxim, that everything

has a cause, the balance between necessity and truth is reversed. This maxim has no logical cogency, but the presumption it expresses is backed by a good deal of evidence. In search of necessity we might correct the statement and say that every *effect* has a cause; but this truism would leave us to consider whether every event is actually an effect.

No actual sequence can be necessary and the sum of causes can have no cause.

Certainly not, unless the series of events runs back to infinity: and even in that case—apart from the heavy strain imposed on human imagination and credulity—the question would arise whether every part of every event was caused by its antecedents, or only its initial phase or its approximate outline. The latter is the plausible view, adopted by Aristotle, and reasonable if we believe in the dominance of a conceptual pattern over the flux of existence. Events will fall into certain classes, animals and their passions will exemplify certain permanent types, but there will be a margin of incalculable variation due to accidental conjunctions or lapses in the execution of the dominant themes. And here again, there are alternative possibilities. These lapses or conjunctions may all have mechanical causes, according to deeper laws of matter, traceable beneath the moral morphology of events; or on the contrary, variations may be free and groundless, though kept within certain bounds by the magic of hereditary types; so that the old equilibrium of the cosmos will right itself after each casual oscillation. Or perhaps these oscillations are casual only in appearance, and from the point of view of their antecedents, while by a secret conspiracy they, or some of them, steadily make for one far-off divine event: and it may have been these successive variations, mechanically uncaused but prophetically inspired, that have created, as it were on the way, the stock genera and species of our transitory world.

These would then be restive in their trammels and destined to be superseded. If all variations and free choices were so directed, they might all be said to have a cause, not in the past, but in the future: and the providential harmony of all the parts and of all the incidents would seem, in one sense, to render them necessary. Not that logically a different issue would not be conceivable, but that morally and emotionally it would be "unthinkable" that any absurd accident should ever come groundlessly to mar so perfect a plan.

Nevertheless, the necessity of each element for the perfection of a particular design confers no necessity upon that design as a whole, nor compels nature to adopt it. Whatever regularity or unity the existing world may exhibit, the existence of such unity or regularity remains a perfectly contingent matter of fact.

But have we not heard of an ontologically necessary Being, the essence of which involves existence? We have heard of it: and this typically meta- *The ontological proof ambiguous.* physical contention brings to a head, and exhibits boldly, the equivocation involved in the idea that any truth is necessarily true. The most real of beings, said St. Anselm, necessarily exists: for evidently if it did not exist, far from being most real, it would not be real at all. Is then reality, we may ask, the same as existence? And can existence have degrees? St. Anselm explains that by greater reality he means more than greater quantity of material being: he means also greater dignity, perfection, and moral greatness. Now, a non-existent essence would woefully lack moral greatness, perfection or dignity: it would be a contemptible ghost, a miserable nothing. Undoubtedly for a care-laden mind seeking salvation—unless it sought salvation from existence—power, which certainly involves existence, must be the first mark of reality and value: what is without power will be without importance. Granting this, the ontological proof is cogent: the most powerful of beings necessarily exists, because power is only another name for the difference which the existence of one thing makes in the existence of another. But a less religious or more practical investigator of power might well come to the conclusion that this greatest, most formidable, and most real of beings was matter, meaning by this not only the substance of interacting things but the principles of their interaction.

At the other pole of reflection, on the contrary, as among the Indians or the Eleatics, the most real of things might seem to be pure Being, or the realm of essence, excluding change and existence altogether: because in change and existence there is essential privation. That from which we lapse or to which we aspire is no longer or not yet; and in being for the moment something in particular we renounce and reject Being in every other form. The truly ontological proof, for a pure ontologist, would therefore assert, not that the most real of beings necessarily exists, but that the most real of beings necessarily does not exist. In other words, reality would be identified with necessary Being, or essence, and this existing world of limitation, contrariety and care would be pronounced an illusion.

I do not mention this paradox in order to laugh at St. Anselm or at his many solemn disciples, but *The word reality, used eulogistically, may indicate essences rather than facts.* precisely to show that behind the sophistry of their words there is, or may be, a secret allegiance to pure and necessary Being. Their play on the word reality perhaps masked an instinctive revolt against worldliness, a desire to throw off somehow the incubus of alien facts and irrational compulsions and find a way back into safety and peace. They called pure Being most real because to their hearts it was most satisfying. Consequently their argument was fallacious and even ridiculous, if by "necessary existence" we understand a necessity attaching to events or to facts, that is, to contingencies. Yet the same argument breathes a fervent intuition and a final judgment of the spirit, if it intends rather to deny final validity to an existential order which, by definition, is arbitrary, treacherous, and self-destructive: a realm of being over which inessential relations are compulsory and essential relations are powerless.

When we are asked to shift the meaning of terms so that, at least in God, essence may involve existence, we are left in doubt as to the direction in which the assimilation is to take place. Are we to idealize existence so that it may be nothing but essence, or to hypostatize essence so as to make it exist? When we speak of being or reality, are we intent on the miracle of existence, and do we pass from that mystery to the conviction that the divine essence is just this miracle, this absolute power, this abysmal fact? Or free from all trouble or wonder, and in placid intellectual clearness, do we first demonstrate to ourselves the necessity and infinity of possible being or essence; so that for us the miracle of existence becomes rather a scandal? For why should innocent and merely possible being be raised for a moment at this or that point into an insane prominence, impossible to sustain or to justify, whilst all the rest of essence is veiled by a passionate ignorance and proclaimed to be nothing? In the latter case, existence would involve privation, partiality, ignorance, instability, and grotesque pride, with a consequent perpetual misery. Instead of the word existence the ontological argument should then employ the word reality, meaning the fullness and indestructibility—*essential indestructibility*—of being.   If we make this substitution, feeling the pregnancy of our terms, we may come to see how the maximum of reality might logically involve infinity, impassiveness, and eternity: all of which are contrary to the limitation, flux, and craving inherent in existence.   No essence, not even this essence of existence, has any power to actualize itself in a fact; nor does such actualization bring to any essence an increment in its logical being; only an alien ambiguous status, no sooner acquired than lost.

The existence of God is therefore not a necessary truth: for if the proposition is necessary, its terms can be only essences; and the word God itself would then designate a definable idea, and would not be a proper name indicating an actual power.   If, on the contrary, the word is such a proper name, and God is a psychological moral being energizing in space and time, then his existence can be proved only by the evidence of these natural manifestations, not by dialectical reasoning upon the meanings of terms.

CHAPTER II

FACTS ARBITRARY, LOGIC IDEAL

THAT one philosopher should profess to have proved some metaphysical tenet, and that another philosopher should profess to have refuted it, might leave the reader cold. It is not in those regions that he ordinarily feels sure of the truth. Are there no truths obviously necessary to common sense? If I have mislaid my keys, *mustn't* they be somewhere? If a child is born, *mustn't* he have had a father? *Must* is a curious word, pregnant for the satirist: it seems to redouble the certainty of a fact, while really admitting that the fact is only conjectured. The necessity asserted foolishly parades the helplessness of the mind to imagine anything different. Yet this helplessness, on which dogmatism rests, is shameful, and is secretly felt to be shameful. Spirit was born precisely to escape such limitations, to see the contingency and finitude of every fact, and to imagine as many alternatives and extensions as possible, some of which may be true, and may put that casual fact in its true setting. Truth is groped after, not imposed, by the presumptions of the intellect: and if these presumptions often are true, the reason is that they are based upon and adjusted to the actual order of nature, which is thoroughly unnecessary, and most miraculous when most regular. This blessed regularity, logically unforeseeable, is indeed the basis of human safety, wisdom, and science; it teaches us what *must* happen under particular circumstances; but accommodation

Physical necessity is conditional on an order of nature itself not necessary.

11

to the truth in these regions leaves the mind, when
not mechanized, full of wonder at the truth.

The mechanized mind, that cannot wonder at the
commonplace, is apt to carry its mechanical presumptions over into logic, as if necessity there
too were simply truth to fact. A large
part of the confidence felt in numerical and
geometrical measurements is an emotional
confidence. It comes from a sense of what would
surely happen to bodies having those numerical or
geometrical properties. We seldom stop to consider
narrowly the logical relations between defined essences,
as pure mathematics would require us to do; but we
rely on common knowledge of the world become in
ourselves an irresistible mode of imagination; and
this precipitation of ideas in ourselves we call necessity
in the object. Anything else would be "impossible":
that is to say, impossible for us to *believe*. Interest
in fact, or confident judgment about fact, here overcomes or confuses interest in essence. Yet wonder
at the commonplace—at the stars or a flower or a
word—comes to almost everybody at certain moments:
because these things are too improbable in themselves
and too inexplicably juxtaposed for a spirit whose
natural field is the perspicuous.

A rationalistic reader might still ask: "Is there
no truth within your realm of essence? Are not
unity and distinctness present in all essences,
and is it not true to say so? And all that
you yourself have written, here and elsewhere, about essence, is it not true?" No,
I reply, it is not true, nor meant to be true.
It is a grammatical or possibly a poetical construction
having, like mathematics or theology, a certain internal
vitality and interest; but in the direction of truth-
finding, such constructions are merely instrumental
like any language or any telescope. A man may fall

*Practical
certainty
mistaken for
logical
necessity.*

*Correctness
or error
within logic
a question
of art, not of
truth.*

into an error in grammar or in calculation. This is a fault in the practice of his art, at bottom a moral defect, a defect in attention, diligence, and capacity: and in my dialectic I have doubtless often clouded my terms with useless or disturbing allusions. But when consistently and conscientiously worked out and stripped to their fighting weight, my propositions will be logically necessary, being deducible from the definitions or intuitions of the chosen terms, and especially of this chosen term "essence" itself. But logic is only logic: and the systems of relation discoverable amongst essences do not constitute truths, but only other more comprehensive essences, within which the related essences figure as parts. The systems, like the logical elements, become a means of expressing truth only when truth can be otherwise discovered and brought face to face with our deductive reasonings. Truth will then domesticate our logic in the world: until perhaps the dialectical guest so hospitably received forgets his essential foreignness and undertakes to drive the poor native facts out of house and home. Our idealisms, in their moral autonomy, can hardly abstain from claiming a divine right to govern the world, to correct it, or at least to scold it for being so unaccountably wrong. And far from right the world indeed is, and must be, judged by human interests and even by human logic, because man and his moral aspirations are only incidents in the universe; but there is one ideal measure that the actual world cannot fall short of: it cannot be far from true.

This truth, if the world had been chaotic, might have excluded the existence of mind altogether, or kept mind down to the sensuous level; but there was a partial rationality or promise of rationality in things that encouraged the mind to clarify its ideas, and to develop logic. Logic is a child of fact, as spirit in general

Double contact of logic with fact.

is a child of the psyche: a headstrong child quick to forget or deny the sweet milk that has nurtured it; yet the bond with earth remains notwithstanding. It remains not only in the past, fundamentally determining the choice of essences that logic shall play with, but it remains also contemporaneously, in that even the logician's thoughts are controlled at every turn by physical accidents and social pressure. It is important to distinguish this nether contact of logic with fact in the biological genetic direction, from the ideal contact established or rather claimed, when logic is used to express or to extend natural knowledge. Biological contact exists also between vital facts and music; it exists between vital facts and illusions, errors, or myths; but music luckily is not expected (until it is coined into language) to convey *knowledge* of facts. That is the secret of its magnificent development: the life of music is free from everything except its natural sources, from everything except the biological impulses and multiple harmonies internal to the organism. Sight and touch, on the contrary, though no less sensuous, animal and subjective than sound, are more readily and completely caught up by the cognitive impulse, and idolatrously treated as *true*: exactly how literally or consistently, it would be endless to trace.

By the truth, as the reader knows, I understand the complete ideal description of existence; and any part of this description will be a truth, that is, a part of the truth. The ideal complete description of an essence, on the contrary, or of the relations between essences, unless this description is rehearsed psychologically by some living mind, is simply that very essence and those very relations: it can be neither false nor true, but only articulate. And the realm of essence being infinite and omnimodal, any other description of any other essence, or relations between

In respect to essences, all definitions are equally valid, since each selects the essence which it defines.

essences, would be equally articulate up to its own degree of elaboration; so that there would be nothing to choose, in the way of truth, between any two descriptions.

This insight removes a problem sometimes needlessly proposed about the choice of definitions, for instance in the case of number or numbers. Mathematicians are unanimous and clear on the point that $2 + 2 = 4$; but they are obscure and divided as to the nature of 2 and of 1, of $+$ and of $=$. And we are allowed to infer that there is a *true* nature of $=$ and $+$, of 1 and of 2. But that, in logic, is nonsense. Each of these essences is whatever it is by *any* definition: the rest is merely a question of names, perhaps preempted by custom to some one definition rather than to another. Essentially, all conceivable natures and definitions are on a par: the only question is historical and psychological, regarding the prevalence of particular notions in the human mind, or else physical, as to the applicability of these notions to the cosmos. In both directions, obscurity is inevitable, and differences of opinion, if modest, are legitimate. It may be expedient to limit the interpretation of mathematical signs to particular humanly chosen ideas: but other interpretations, perhaps less fertile or useful, would not be essentially less cogent. Truth, then, never enters the field of mathematics at all; and there is no *true* view about the nature of number or numbers, until the discussion veers from mathematics altogether, to physics, history or psychology.

From this it follows that we may intelligently adopt and apply the category of truth to current perceptions and opinions, inasmuch as they profess to be knowledge and are asserted of positive facts: but when, in reflection, we make some supposition deliberately contrary to fact, the relevance of truth to that supposition is exhausted before we begin to develop it.

Suppositions contrary to fact also transcend the realm of truth.

The supposition is admittedly false; and in consider-
ing it further we are exploring the relations it may
have in the realm of essence only, where questions
of truth do not arise.   Romantic people think of what
might have been: some danger narrowly escaped,
some bet almost won: possibilities near enough to
the truth to seem false, and perhaps bitter.   In this
moodiness we may say that the poets lie: but the
poets did not lie, they were inspired.   Their suppositions were contrary to fact only by accident, and quite
apart from their innocent intention.   No doubt common waking perception is truer than poetry, and the
poets in their sane moments will not deny it: but
inspiration liberates them from that interest.   The
crucial point is this: that not only are all particular
truths and facts contingent, but the very categories of
fact and truth, like all other essences, if they are
exemplified at all, are exemplified unnecessarily and
by a groundless chance.

Logic, when once its foothold in fact has been
secured at any point, has a moral part to play, and
Contact   this in two directions.   It humanizes the
with truth   world, since we now can think and reason
adds moral
value to   about it with some relevance; and it vivifies
logic.   speculation, by allying the furthest reaches
of it with real life.   Logic traces the radiation of
truth: I mean that when one term of a logical system
is known to describe a fact, the whole system attach-
able to that term becomes, as it were, incandescent,
and forms a part of the aura of truth.   The terms of
logic are themselves originally glimpses of facts: we
deepen this apprehension humanly and morally when
we develop ideally the qualities which a fact truly
wears either in itself or in relation to human faculties
and interests; as a poet deepens his sense of beauty,
if one beauty in his mind recalls another, and he
finds metaphors and musical words that may re-echo

his passion. But we may also deepen our apprehension by buttressing it with apprehensions of kindred or neighbouring facts, which though interlopers in that argument, support it by analogy or qualify its value. Here is where allusions, logically redundant, may help to brighten the faint rays of truth still colouring high speculation. Between the branchings of our logic, that spread aloft forgetful of the truth in which, after all, they are remotely rooted, we may catch fresh glimpses of earth and sky, and so gain, as we go, circumstantial support or correction for our deductions.

Thus grammar, rhetoric, and logic enrich enormously the phenomenon of being alive. They embroider every image with a thousand latent analogies and concordant rhymes; and they enshrine this image in the ideal world to which, after all, every image belongs. Because the truth or applicability of ideas, as of words, though it may be the chief or only source of their importance, is irrelevant to their sensuous or intrinsic character: so that when an idea, weighted with the dignity of truth, is lifted out again from the alien context and accidental occasion which allied it with fact, that idea seems to be clarified and to sing hallelujah; for it finds itself free at last to be itself, and to trace its internal affinities in its native element. Nor is this merely a sensual or logical holiday for the mind: it is a holiday or holy day also in a religious sense; because weighted with truth as the idea now is, it drags, as it were, the whole workaday world with it into the light. The world which was but a too familiar fact suddenly becomes beautiful: and at the same time the idea, only a graphic pattern before, now touches the heart and becomes poetical.

And lends it a tragic force.

Finally, turning the doctrine here defended against itself, we might ask whether it is not necessarily true

that the truth is contingent and not necessary. Here
again I must repeat that what is necessary logically
is not necessarily *true*. In this case, that truth
is contingent is a necessary proposition,
because facts, by definition, make the truth
true and all facts, again by definition, are
contingent. But there is no necessity in the choice
or in the applicability of such categories as necessity,
truth, or fact. These categories are not necessarily
true. I find that, as a matter of fact, they are true,
or at least true enough: they articulate human thought
in a normal way which reality on the whole seems to
sanction. They are the lungs and heart-valves of the
mind. And while we use these categories, we shall
be obliged on pain of talking nonsense to stick to
their connotations, and to acknowledge, among other
things, that there are no necessary truths. But the
possession of such categories is after all a psychological
or even a personal accident; and the fact that they
are convenient, or even absolutely true in describing
the existing world, is a cosmic accident.

My own logic, even if made cogent, not therefore true.

The thesis of the first chapter, then, that there are
no necessary truths, is itself made necessary only by
virtue of certain assumed intuitions or
definitions which fix the meaning of the
terms necessity, contingency, existence, and
truth. But no definition and no intuition
can render true the term that it distinguishes. My
thesis will therefore be a true thesis only in so far
as in the realm of existence facts may justify my
definitions and may hang together in the way that
those definitions require. The case is the same in
principle as in the homely equation, $2 + 2 = 4$; only
that in arithmetic the terms are simpler and more
familiar, so that the necessary relation between them
is obvious to more people. It happens at the same
time that the application of arithmetic, where it applies,

It is true only in so far as it is applicable.

is most constant and exact, so that its truth in those regions is beyond doubt; whereas any general logic applied to describing the universe, however ancient and well tried this logic may be, remains rather a form of human grammar. We are in a region of free intuition and construction, as in music, with no claims to propounding a revealed or a revealing truth.

CHAPTER III

INTERPLAY BETWEEN TRUTH AND LOGIC

HAVING laid down this distinction between logic and truth, and shown that truth, as I define it, is wholly

There is a contingent, I have no desire to quarrel with
kind of truth mankind for using words as they choose,
internal to and talking of truth also in cases where
discourse,
depending there is only consistency. There is much
on fidelity. truth, even in my sense, possible in respect
to ideas: not only psychological and historical truth, in describing the ideas that may have actually arisen in the human mind, but also formal truth in the description of an accepted idea in terms different from those in which it was couched at first; a change in expression which may serve to analyse that idea and bring out its essential affinities. Mathematics, logic, and a certain kind of psychology may thus create a phenomenological science; that is, a faithful description of some field of essence already selected and duly named; and we must allow that, at least according to the genius of the English language, whatever is faithful and trusty may be called true.

This idiomatic use of the word true is semi-moral. It turns on not belying one's professions and being constant to a plighted troth. Serious thought requires this sort of fidelity. We begin by noticing and liking some idea, and the very earnestness of our attention becomes a pledge in our own minds not to drop that idea, nor adulterously to slip another idea in its place. Truth—truth to it and to ourselves—now demands

that we make it clearer and clearer, more and more
unmistakable; and perhaps, by an illusion not unknown to lovers, we attribute to our first intuition
a prophetic force, as if it had irresistibly predestined
us to these later developments.   But ideas, if by ideas
we mean essences and not impressions, are as Berkeley
termed them, inert.   They do not compose a world
but a vocabulary: and their logical relations, though
immutable, have no aggressive force compelling us to
notice them.   We evoke ideas for a moment of our
own motion; and they vanish like sounds and shadows,
without leaving a trace.   Thus if our intuition had
been careless and not vitally rooted, the essence evoked
in passing would never have been retained or recovered
adequately in a second intuition.   Its fleeting definiteness for sense would never have become an express
definition for thought.   In dismissing and forgetting
that image we should then be committing no infidelity.
Obviously we could never falsify our old ideas if we
never thought of them again.

    This drift of ideation, however, which would be
innocent if it were purely sensuous, may invade dialectic and explicit recollection, becoming a   Infidelity to
perpetual fountain of sophistry.   Each time   a first
we mention a word we may give it a different   meaning is
                                                 sometimes
meaning, and the more we shift and vary,   called dia-
the deeper we may think we go.   We lie,   lectic, and
                                             may adjust
either idly or maliciously, when we allow   ideas to
invention to transform our memories; and   facts.
we contradict ourselves if we allow invention or the
flux of accidental thought to vitiate the sense of our
original terms.   Dialectic then becomes, as in Hegel,
a romantic alternation of ideal or moral impulses.
Infidelity to one's thoughts is here felt to be truth
to one's deeper self and to one's destiny; and it may
really be so when the thin pretence to logic covers a
shrewd perception of the instability of life.   For there

are mental reservations and insincerities hiding in our
explicit assertions, treasons latent in our promises, and
unforeseen social currents destined to carry our
thoughts suddenly in new directions. All this may
make excellent dramatic history or phenomenology of
morals; and if it seems to skirt dangerously a Mephisto-
phelean abyss of mockery and biting scorn, it may be
rendered unexpectedly edifying by the assurance that
our dead selves are stepping-stones to higher things,
that the sum of illusions is the only truth, and that a
sufficient experience of folly produces wisdom, not by
repentance, but by approximation. Yet even suppos-
ing that this romantic idealism truly represented the
facts, in calling this description of the facts logic we
should be turning the irony of logic upon logic itself;
and dialectic, far from developing faithfully the implications of ideas, would glorify the infidelities of
things to those ideas.

Whether glorious or feeble these infidelities are
inevitable, since things are in flux and ideas, in the
History logical sense, are unchangeable. Moreover,
laughs at there is necessarily some novel idea or pat-
politics. tern illustrated in the flux itself, and a
special trope in each turn of affairs; so that the truth
of history perpetually gives the lie to the maxims of
men, and defeats their politics and ambition. Yet
looked at from outside, with the wisdom that comes
after the fact, people's actions may seem to the historian to have been directed upon the ends actually
achieved; whereas in fact the result was unintended
and probably unforeseen; though it is easier to foresee
the future than to command it, and only those seem
to command it who pre-figure it with enthusiasm.
Infinitely deeper than the logic of our thoughts is the
fertility of our destiny; and circumstances keep us
alive by continually defeating us. In strictness no
man ever succeeds: the only question is whether he

shall be defeated by the action of others or by his own action.

The notion that history might be dialectical would hardly have seemed plausible to anybody, had not dialectic been conceived in a satirical sense; as when each speaker in a dialogue refutes the others, and the argument ends in the refutation of everybody. The author in such a case speaks for nature, and laughs at opinions. If he is candid he even laughs at his own opinion, and what he exhibits in his dialectic is not logic triumphant but logic losing itself in the sea of fact.

Nor is captious disputation requisite to this end. So long as logic is not thoroughly purified and abstracted, but is applied to things, a man's most honest ideas may issue in the same contrariety. Existence is once for all irrational and cannot be wholly elucidated in terms of essence. And since, at the same time, it is only in terms of essence that facts can be described, partiality and instability beset all description. If a thing is small, it is also large, compared with something smaller. If it is good, it is also bad; if true also false. Nor does this hold only of relatives. If a thing has being, or definite character, it also lacks being, because in being what it is it rejects and banishes all that it is not, so that all positive wealth is shadowed by privation.

Ontological divergence between logic and fact.

This famous union of opposites, philosophers being naturally rapt in the excitement of assertion and not having time to be quite honest, gives rise to no less famous fallacies. A first fallacy is this: that the relativity and self-disruption found in the description of facts is transferred to the terms of the description, that is, to the essences confronting each other there. But these essences have no inherent ambiguity

The union of contraries in things imports no contradiction into essences.

or tendency to pass into their opposites. Large has no proclivity to mean small, good to mean bad, or true false, or wealth privation, or being not-being. If each of these essences could alienate its character, they could not remain terms in consistent assertions; they could not be so much as compared or opposed, and all discourse and perception would sink into black night. It is only in describing half-hidden, complex, substantial facts that ambiguities and contradictions appear; for here essences essentially different (since each is invincibly itself) are found alternately or simultaneously present. Were the essences not still different and absolutely fixed in character, there would be no problem in their co-presence, and no dialectic: only a flow of indistinguishables, if so much as a flow could be distinguished.

It may be noted in passing that essences are not intrinsically predicates or adjectives, but primordial and distinct forms of possible being. They become predicates or adjectives when an animal psyche apprehending them is vitally preoccupied with the pressure of matter, and with reacting upon that pressure; so that the given essences are taken for portions or qualities of the dynamic fact by which the psyche is confronted. Save for that material preoccupation, the spirit would regard the essences evoked before it in their intrinsic characters as the adequate furniture of life for the moment, like an eagle in repose observing the sun. Moreover, pure Being is not a substance in which individual essences inhere, so that the essences might be predicates of it. Pure Being is itself only an essence. Expressly, it is that which all essences have in common—namely, character or distinguishableness and self-identity; but pregnantly, pure Being covers the whole realm of essence or the sum of all essences, since all essences are needed to display fully all that

The nature of pure Being recalled.

is self-identical and distinguishable, and that has being or character.

A second fallacy incidental to the dialectic of opposites suggests a superstitious origin. Contradiction (which exists only in human language describing facts that in themselves cannot be contradictory) is transferred to the facts themselves, as if a moral uneasiness existed in them compelling them to shift their ground. Heraclitus seems to have hinted at something of the sort, in his oracular fashion: we learn that war is the parent of all things, and that justice or punishment condemns everything definite to destruction, as if it were a sin to be finite. In Hegel the same pantheistic sentiment was doubtless reinforced by intimate acquaintance with self-contradiction and self-dissolution in Protestant theology. Here sometimes there may really have been an uneasy conscience and a conflict of contrary feelings driving the mind to the next stage of enlightenment, and from that stage on. Yet the progress of dialectic even in this field, where there was a primary contradiction between tradition and enquiry, has suffered many reversals and has taken a long time. Not the logic of the beliefs, but the ripeness of society or of private sentiment for a change of view has determined the direction of reform and the halting-places of opinion. In general, it is fabulous to represent phenomenology, or the drama of ideas, as the motive force in history. Phenomena are inert results, æsthetic figments: while the derivation of event from event is a natural flow, with crises and cataclysms here and there, but for the most part lapsing with a serene monotony and a tireless self-repetition. This steady underlying vortex of nature keeps mankind alive and keeps it human: which does not prevent civilizations and empires from rising and falling, not always by mutual conflict

Natural instability represented mythically as logical contradiction.

or direct succession, but often by some local accretion
of martial and social energy, vegetating spontaneously,
as the Greeks and the Romans vegetated, and sucking
their neighbours up into their more vigorous organism,
not at all by dialectic. Nor is it dialectic, or any
new idea, that commonly destroys the victor in his
turn; ruin comes by the dissolution of his fighting
organization and the changed habits that his very
victory leads him to form. We may personify these
habits in a miracle play, and show how virtues and
vices rule the destinies of nations. Heraclitus had
said so too: every man's character is his dæmon,
presiding over his fate. And this interplay of the
causes of life and death we may call, if we like, the
dialectic of existence.

In Hegel's miracle play there are indeed many
stretches of genuine logic, where he dissects the meanings of given ideas. Such analysis clarifies
its own terms, and no cataclysms of nature
or opinion can annul the validity of the
deductions made from those terms logically.
Whether the deduction is logical or empirical and
arbitrary can be tested by this circumstance: that true
analysis leaves the original idea whole and uncon-
taminated, in the centre of all the radiating ideas that
may be brought to surround it: whereas in a psychological flux, as in a dream, additions transform the
original datum, identifications are fallacious, progress
is made through oblivion, and the whole torrent is
lost in sand. Yet as the sand itself is a quicksand, and
moves, the romantic historian sees nothing tragic in
the evaporation of his original stream: there will
always be something on foot to undergo interesting
transformations. Hegel's attention was accordingly
not long arrested on pure analysis. Analysis served
chiefly to loosen ideas, and open some breach for
destructive criticism. The point was to produce a

pregnant confusion in which the logician might drop the thread of his argument and pick up some contrary fact. The air of this dialectic is thick with the fumes of earth; this makes its strength and its charm; and such a picture of mutation, by its very homeliness and allegiance to truth, confirms my contention that truth and logical necessity are independent things.

Pleasant as well as tragic is the perpetual excitement of finding that which there was no reason to expect. If our prudence is discouraged, our vitality is stimulated; and existence, for the romantic soul, becomes a Gothic marvel, infinitely extensible in quality and quantity, unmapped and incalculable. If any eternal fitness seems nevertheless attributable to the course of things, this fitness will lie entirely in an occasional æsthetic or religious emotion arising during the process itself. *Romantic chaos.*

The taste for chaos, however, is hardly normal, because even in the act of demanding chaos the mind throws out a postulate that, by a secret necessity, this chaos shall never lapse into order. And what assurance can the empirical observer or pure experimenter possess that the indetermination he observes is not specious, and due to the superficial external cognizance which he takes of events? Might there not be a rationality in them hidden from his eyes? And, indeed, it is almost inevitable that, among events which interest him and remain in his memory, there should exist some mutual relevance. Every event, though unnecessary and spontaneous, will probably be pertinent to what went before, as each fresh episode in a serial story, unexpected as it may be to the reader, must somehow be grafted upon the previous characters and episodes. Even to break in and interrupt an experience, events must have a certain dramatic continuity, and fall into a temporal and moral order in *Any view of reality when taken to be true becomes imposing.*

the mind that records them.   This psychological compulsion soon generates superstitions and prophecies about the secretly meaningful and fatal order of events; and the supposed paths of destiny are explored with as much intellectual ardour and foretaste of truth as were ever the laws of nature.

Cognitive ambition, on the physical side, is inherent in hunting and fighting; and on the spiritual side and for reflection it involves something like a taste for truth.   To be deceived is as hateful to the mind as it is dangerous to the body. Impatience and vanity, however, at once intervene; so that it is not facts so much that. dominate human knowledge, in its sweep and intensity, as imagination that lends importance and felt reality to alleged facts. Impetuous thought is then led to claim a double truth: one sort of truth legitimately, truth to inspiration; and another sort of truth abusively, truth to fact.   The vital and moral heat inseparable from thinking thus often renders logic dogmatic, and seduces it from its ideal cogency to posing as material truth. The mathematician has this justification, that his original data are simple and true.   They have been tested and clarified in daily life from time immemorial; so that his speculative superstructure has a certain diminishing affinity or relevance to material truth, apart from its logical validity.   Yet the glory of his science does not reside, for him, in that link with contingent fact, but rather in a certain almost humorous compulsiveness in its logical development: whence its reputation for certitude (not merited in the higher reaches of his speculation) which can make it, even for an empiricist like Locke, the ideal of knowledge.

Here, however, the pride of mathematics, like that of theology, comes before a fall.   There is no end of science, no end of learning, in both pursuits; but mathematics, like theology, is not knowledge of any-

Natural origin of dogmatism.

thing but itself. *True* knowledge, *natural* knowledge, should be the cognizance that one existing thing takes of another; and this perforce is a form of faith, though justified in continual physical contacts between the knower and the known: whereas mathematics and theology trace ideal relations for their own sake and end in the air.

The bad repute into which logic fell at the Renaissance, for being tautological, might at any moment overtake mathematics, were it not for the utility of mathematics in the applied arts. For in themselves the higher mathematics, in spite of their exactitude, or because of it, have not the direct savour of truth. They are scholastic, they are almost occult; and the hearty shrewd lover of truth distrusts such acrobatic marvels. What he trusts is experiment, exploration, and the warm immediacy of action and passion in his own person; he would like to laugh at all abstract speculation as the most ridiculous of shams. And he would be right in laughing, if logic or mathematics pretended to truth: but that is a claim foisted on them by the dogmatism of common perception, contrary to their proper genius. It is like the claim to truth or utility foisted by pedagogues on the fine arts. Philosophy has too long been pedagogical, and the best schooldays are half-holidays. If liberty has opened a window for us towards the infinite realm of essence, it has not authorized us to regard the prospect visible to us there as the truth about nature. Much less are we authorized to set up our visions as moral standards to which things ought to conform. The order of subordination is the opposite one. Nature being what she is, and we being in consequence what we are, certain special reaches of essence are obvious to our senses and intellect. Sights and sounds, pains and pleasures assail us; and our leisure is free to develop

Logic, when turned into metaphysics, spoils both physics and logic.

in music and language, in mathematics and religion, the moral burden of our animal existence. Nor will this play of ideas be sheer truancy. Our toys may become instruments, our sensations signs; and a part of the truth about nature and about ourselves will be necessarily revealed to us, directly or indirectly, by the mere existence and sequence of those apparitions. Directly, in emotion, perception, and dramatic sympathy, we may learn to know the human world, the world of images, morals, and literature: and indirectly, in close connection with the flow of sensation, we may learn to posit permanent objects and to pick our way among them to good purpose, as a child finds his way home.

CHAPTER IV

PSYCHOLOGICAL APPROACHES TO TRUTH

EVEN if mathematical ideas were less exactly true of the world, the mere possession of them would be indirect evidence that they had some cognitive value and were in some way true. If we would show them to be false, we must propose other ideas on the same subject which shall seem truer. But what ideas, truer than those of mathematical physics, can we propose on the subject of the field of action or the dynamic world? Undoubtedly, if reality were confined to spiritual being, mathematics would be useless, and the study of it an idle pastime, if not a vice; and if any spiritual man, like Pascal, got too deeply entangled in mathematics, the sad effects might be seen in his self-torture and desperation. A faith founded on logic is an acrobatic and insane faith. It was not logical necessity, but hard practical evidence, that first suggested mathematical ideas to the mind and afterwards confirmed and imposed them. Animal faith honours mathematical science—a fantastic construction in itself —for measuring reliably the footsteps of that stealthy material power that pervades the world. If mathematics measures these footsteps perfectly, mathematics is perfectly true. The reality of psychologists—subjective presence, whether sensuous or conceptual— belongs to a different moral or æsthetic sphere, not mediated by animal faith and not itself conveying knowledge of truth, true as the account of such experi-

All ideas have some expressive rightness.

ence may be which is conveyed later by memory or
sympathetic fancy: for often the art of fiction may
tell us the truth about the fictions natural to the
mind.

Nevertheless, intuition, which is simply sensibility
focussed and actually noticing anything, comes upon
They are   essences, not things: because in proportion
biological   as attention takes notice, and honestly
products and   observes what it finds, it suspends that
spontane-
ously   animal faith which was involved in fear or
poetical.   care or the physical impulse to react upon
some physical stimulus.   When clarified and thoroughly actualized, all data are essences: if the spirit
could actualize and clarify everything it would live
altogether in its congenial ideal world, as it does, with
some lingering qualifications, in mathematics and
poetry and music.   But in animal life this remains an
interlude, something marginal and ulterior.   Living
attention comes upon essences with a bias, from some
particular vital angle: they are stepping-stones in a
distracted career.   Even if clearly focussed in their
own plane, essences do not dictate to us in what
direction their relations shall be traced: in themselves
they have no movement, no selectiveness, no pro-
pulsion.   The choice of this or that path, in further
intuition, is made by the animal mind, under suasion
of casual interests or its own vegetative growth.
Poetry does not make itself, poets must make it: and
so mathematicians must make mathematics.   Narrow
paths are thus opened by accident through the compact thicket of essential Being; and later comers,
threading the beaten way, may suppose that they are
surveying the whole structure of the labyrinth, and
discovering the eternal Logos, or self-chosen necessary
truth.   But the labyrinth, being infinite, offers all
choices to the wanderer; and the pattern actually
traced was selected by accident.

Logic is a refined form of grammar. If in my prattle I obey a tendency, and later establish a rule to the effect that nouns shall be either masculine or feminine; and if I obey a tendency and make it a rule that adjectives shall match and prolong the gender of their substantives; *then* it is requisite for propriety of speech that adjectives and nouns should possess gender, and should march in couples, like clerical school children, the girls with girls, and the boys with boys. And this contrast, with this divided way of trooping together, artificial as it is in things without sex, opens the way to the most charming assonances and beckonings of word to word in discourse, enabling us without confusion to pick our way through a minuet of cross-references, as in an ode of Horace. Yet grammar need never have adopted so fantastic a sexual analogy. It did so only because speech is radically expletive, redundant, and exclamatory, as thought is also; and in a creature to whom sexual images are arresting and highly provocative, sexual analogies, however far-fetched, will appear in all sorts of places, particularly when emotion is aroused, and will count for more in the play of description than does the strict truth of the object.

Grammar is biassed (1) by emotional associations.

There are other graver intrusions of the grammatical medium into the deliverance of thought. For instance, the relation of subject to predicate is founded on the circumstance that some words are proper names, and merely demonstrative, like a pointing finger; other words are names of essences, without traceable physical being, but appearing dispersed, repeated, and mysteriously intermittent in all sorts of places or in no place at all, that is to say, in the mind. The proper name, indicating and holding down, as it were, the physical object that concerns us

(2) By the external approach of thought to things, producing a dualism of subject and predicate.

in action, becomes the grammatical subject; and the names of such essences as this subject shares with other things become grammatical predicates and adjectives. This grammar registers admirably the education of the mind: for the mind is commonly awakened by some shock, and then proceeds more or less scrupulously to describe the circumstances and the qualities connected with that stimulus.

Moreover, being a spirit beset by animal obsessions, the human mind can retain, compare, and synthesize (3) By its impressions, leaving the flux of existence synthesis in to run on as full and turbid as it will. Yet sensation, perception, this recollection and this withdrawal are and memory. always imperfect. The basis of spirit is itself material, fluid, and self-forgetful: while on the other hand, the knowledge gathered and the pictures painted by the mind are simplified unduly, convention-alized, moralized, reduced to types: and this does violence to the truth, since nature is not human educa-tion hypostatized. Hence the quarrel between the humanities and science; in which science evidently represents the interests of truth. If the problem were scientific, we should have to consider that science also is human, that neither in texture nor in scope can science be identified with the truth: and that the humanities too convey poetical information about historical matters. But the real problem is moral; and even if science presented the truth more honestly than the humanities, we should still have to ask whether these scientific truths were the most important, and even whether the knowledge of truth is the ultimate goal or good of mind. Frankly, it is not, when the mind is free. Spirit is the entelechy or ultimate fruit of life and not a material instrument or means to action; and if once life were safely adjusted and directed amid material circumstances, consciousness of those circum-stances would be superfluous except as it might be interesting; so that truth would take its place side by side with fiction of every sort, to be valued not because true—for merely being true does not make things worth knowing—but only for invigorating and entertaining the mind. Such is the liberal life; and the humanities have this liberal character, although science also has it, in so far as the truth of it enlarges the imagination. But such poetic freedom in thinking is premature, and even criminal, when the psyche is living at cross-purposes with the possibilities of life. Health must be established first and organized securely; and then the range and balance of spiritual interests may be left for free genius to determine.

In any case, it would be a vain scruple in the lover of truth to quarrel with his intellect and with the grammar of his thoughts in order to put his ear closer to the ground. His ear is itself an animal organ, and its deliverance—sound —is the substance of nothing except music. The tread of oncoming reality may be conveyed more impressively or more accurately by one sense than by another: but in the end only intellect and science will be able to reveal the method of that approaching attack, or the method of meeting it by any deliberate or artificial contrivance. There is no ground for deprecating this intervention of art and reason. Mind is better than matter in the estimation of mind: and this judgment is final, because only mind is capable of esteeming or judging at all. Attention to matter is therefore optional for a moral being, and important only when, health having been lost, art is requisite for recovering it; or when, as I was saying just now, attention to matter is spontaneous and self-rewarding, as it is for children and for the true naturalist. The office of matter is precisely to breed mind and to feed it; and while the fantastic egotistical errors into which mind

This bias legitimate: because mind, though dependent physically, is autonomous morally.

D

may fall, since it must conceive matter in terms of ideas, might seem laughable to omniscience, those errors do no harm to matter and very little to mind. An unbiassed and literal understanding of matter would be incongruous in an animal; and for pure spirit such understanding remains an ulterior speculative ambition, legitimate certainly, since spirit is potentially omniscient, but rather beside the mark when, being incarnate, that spirit is beset by impurities which it must purge first, before it can ever understand anything or know itself. If it knew itself, spirit would be little pressed to understand the depths of matter, which cannot be changed; but spirit, by existing, does lend to matter a new mental dimension, expressing material organization morally and perhaps gloriously. Better than idly mirroring nature in mind (if it were possible to do so) is to impose an ideal measure upon fluid things, and this not arbitrarily or insignificantly: for the very dependence of spirit, which might seem to condemn it to futility, renders it an index to deeper realities and an organ of truth. Thought would never arise or maintain itself, it would never succeed in imposing formal measures and unities on events, if these events, which include the biological organs of thought, were not already organized and self-distinguished in the bosom of chaos. The very existence of fiction endows fiction with a native relevance to truth.

We are told by certain psychologists that although the dynamic order of events is not *really* mathematical, mathematical fictions must be cultivated because they are *useful in the practical arts*. But why should they be useful if false? And how should they be false if they describe the efficacious order of nature, by which our existence and health and power of speech and thought are notoriously controlled? What better criterion have we of truth than pertinence to action and implica-

Alleged utility of scientific falsifications.

tion in the dynamic order of nature? Primitive imagination no doubt attributes power to wishes and prayers or to formal rhymes and coincidences in the aspects of things; but that is superstition; and we gradually discover the true order of nature by attentive observation of matter, and experiments with it, and calculation of its quantity and movement. If arithmetical and geometrical notions gain such ascendancy over the expert mind, it is precisely because, in their abstraction, they are the surest measure of the concrete. By them we retrace the actual vectors of reality and energy in the living world. What the vitalists call life is, in comparison, but the after-taste and rhetoric of motion.

Irrelevant, then, as the inner cogency of logic may be to the truth, logic nevertheless possesses a natural truth in its first notions, in its chief lines of deduction, and in many of its developments. Such applicability rewards later speculation for the early diligence of mankind in study- ing material things, turning and moulding them, and making their image precise in thought. Ideas are not true because they are clear, but often they have become clear because they were true. This truth gives continual encourage- ment to the dialectitian in tracing his deductions and trusting his insights. Yet he goes too far when with these ideas, framed on the human scale and true and empirically tested on that scale, he presumes to fathom the depths of matter and of time, and to dictate to nature the mechanism of her motions. He ought rather to expect that in some dimensions of being, for instance, in the mind, or at a high degree of complica- tion, as in living bodies, the applicability of his ideal science should cease to be perfect or should fail altogether. Not that in those regions there is less order than in the gross mechanical world: there is

Mind, without copying or limiting truth, naturally and poetic- ally conforms to it.

evidently more, and a more organic order: but our images and thoughts are not easily adapted to those latitudes and longitudes, and the most signal instances of responsiveness in events seem to us miracles or accidents.

Such limitations are not a fault in human logic or mathematics, as if mankind had been bewitched and ought to begin thinking with other images and other axioms. Even if such a reform of the intellect were possible, and fresh ideal systems were developed, expressly to fit the regions newly explored, the new logic and mathematics would not be likely to fit all reality, or to possess more than a limited and borrowed truth. Nature, we must never forget, is in flux. This flux may move in any number of streams, according to any variety of methods; and even if, at one time, we had obtained an exact formula for everything, presently the flux might take a new turn, and insensibly change its fluid constitution. Then the very accuracy of our earlier measures would render them worthless in a later world.

CHAPTER V

RADIATION OF TRUTH

WE have seen that the truth, as I take the word, is subservient to existence: it is ontologically secondary and true of something else. Yet that which is generated by existence may be itself ideal, and often must be so; because the flux of existence is blind and precipitates a thousand accidents of form by merely flowing, accidents supervening on all the material factors concerned in generating them. Truth itself is such a supervening form; not accidental in the sense of being avoidable, since by existing the world fatally determines the truth about itself; but accidental in the sense of adding, at no expense of matter or energy, an impalpable eternal dimension to transitory being. Events did not intend, so to speak, to be recorded; yet in the truth they have left their unintentional mark, their indelible portrait. Even if things escape observation, they cannot escape having been what they were.

Physical being generates ideal relations.

Existence, as it inevitably generates truth, may on special occasions also generate beauty or goodness, but not with the same pervasiveness. Beauty and goodness are far more accidental than truth: they arise only at certain junctures, when various streams of events, already flowing in definite tropes, meet and mingle in a temporary harmony; a harmony which such of these streams as are organized into psyches may feel and rejoice in. Truth, on the other hand, arises by automatic radiation from every region of fact; since no

39

event can occur without rendering it eternally true
that such an event and no other fills that point of space
and time.

Now as truth, although in itself only a field of
essence, radiates from contingent fact, and is determined and limited by it, so truth itself
establishes certain harmonies and distinctions dominating the realm of thought.
For thought is originally aroused by events,
and directed upon them: it is indicative, and *takes
notice*, as we say of young children when their intelligence is dawning. Even when most slumberous and
vegetative, consciousness, at least in man, is always
partly cognitive, and therefore interested in the truth.
Truth thus becomes the arbiter of success in one of
the most important functions of life: that of intelligent
adjustment on the part of living beings to the conditions under which they live. This adjustment is
physical; but the token of it for the spirit comes in
foresight, sane imagination, and sentiments pertinent
to the facts. In so far as consciousness can become
more than vain sensation or blind anguish, it must
therefore aspire to possess the truth. The truth will
be declared, however partially, by any opinion that
prophesies an event before this event arises, or describes
it when occurring, or reports it after it has occurred.
Such opinions are all incidental to the truth: they may
be framed or not, according to the accidents of human
life and intelligence. They reproduce the truth in
part, as it may be discoverable from their various
stations with their various organs; but the truth in its
wholeness outruns and completes their several deliverances, and is the standard which these deliverances
conform to, in so far as they are true.

This possible discovery of truth, or of some part of
the truth, is often confused with truth itself; as if
truth were like error, the moral quality of some idea

*Truth in
turn sub-
tends intelli-
gence.*

or judgment, when the latter succeeds or (in the case of error) fails to report the fact to which attention for the moment is directed. But an idea or judgment is only true if it reports the truth, and false if it contradicts the truth. That which is true is the proposition, relation, or other essence actually illustrated in the facts. If this proposition, relation, or other essence is asserted in a judgment the judgment *That which is true in ideas or judgments in what they say, not what they are.*
is true by participation, because it speaks the truth. This participation of true judgment in the truth is neither an ontological reproduction by the judgment (which is an invisible act of the mind) of the object (which may be anything whatever); nor is it a vital compatibility of this judgment with all other judgments on all other subjects. Not the assertion as a psychological fact is true, but only that which it asserts: and the difference in quality and value between true ideas and false ideas, taken as states of mind, is a moral difference: the true ideas being safer and probably clearer and more humorous than the false, and marking a success on the mind's part in understanding the world, whereas false ideas would mark a failure. But even this moral quality of enlightening or deceiving us is not an intrinsic passive quality in true or false ideas; as if any clear and distinct idea were true, and any vague sensation or sentiment false. The opposite is often the case; because a scent, olfactory or intellectual, may be a true scent and may truly discriminate objects in their most important practical relations; whereas the clearest and most distinct images and definitions may be definitions and images of mere essences, and not at all true.

The term "idea", in this connection, is trebly ambiguous. It may mean an essence, the theme or internal object of a feeling or thought. It may also mean the feeling or thought, the moment of living

intuition in which such an essence may be distinguished.   Finally, it may mean a feeling or thought
"Ideas",   raised to the self-transcendent value of a
whether   belief or judgment, affirming the given
essences,   essence to be true of some further object.
intuitions,
or judg-   In this last sense, an idea means an opinion,
ments,   and may be called true or false by assimilation
are never
true intrin-   or contrariety to the truth of its object.   But
sically.   an idea that is an innocent feeling or thought,
asserting nothing, cannot be true or false: it is a pure
intuition of an essence.   Much less can the essences
given in such intuition be true or false in themselves.
They may have been raised elsewhere to the plane of
truth, by being exemplified in events: they are not
rendered true by being evoked in intuition, as all falsehoods and all fancies are evoked also.   An idea, therefore, in the third sense of opinion, can be true or false
only if it reports or contradicts some part of the truth:
and in order to do this it must be other than an inert
essence, and more than a pure feeling or thought.   It
must be a judgment affirming a given essence of an
ulterior object, in which that essence may, in truth,
be exemplified or not exemplified.

Truth, then, though descriptive of existence, has
no existence of its own, and remains an ideal standard
Nor do   for any opinions professing to be somewhat
"ideas" be-   true, or true as far as they go.   The empirical
come true
by virtue of   relations which an opinion, by the action it
their rela-   comports, may have in the world have
tion as events
to other   nothing to do with its truth.   If an "idea"
events.   is useful, it is useful, not true: and if an
idea is beautiful or comforting, it is not therefore true,
but comforting only or beautiful; and if an idea, perhaps an illusion, is harmonious with another idea, the
two are harmonious, and both together may be a
worse illusion than each of them was separately.   Nor
would perfect coherence in ideas, in the longest of

dreams, make the dream true; although if it contained intelligent mutual descriptions of one part of it by another part, those parts would indeed report a part of the truth about one another. Yet the total truth about that dream, as some parts of it might perhaps perceive, would be that it was a dream and all sheer illusion. To reduce truth to coherence is to deny truth, and to usurp that name for a certain comfort and self-complacency in mere thinking. Why trouble about truth, if I can be sure of never discovering my error?

Here we see that curious self-degradation which is latent in egotism. You seem to be making your self and your experience absolute; yet by that very arrogance you cut yourself off from all intellectual dominion over anything else, and renounce the very thought of natural knowledge or genuine truth. And this fate overtakes the empiricist or pragmatist no less than the absolute idealist who frankly admits it, and thinks it the proof of his essential divinity. A desultory experience might indeed contain true thoughts about its own progress, physics being strictly reduced, for the philosopher, to literary psychology. This would allow truth an absolute standing in the fields of psychology and history, and all opinions of historians and psychologists would acknowledge that absolute truth as their standard. But such is not the position of radical or romantic empiricists, who are bent on denying that there is truth about futures, or any fixed truth about the past, each historian making a new "truth", in framing a fresh perspective. Transcendental egotism, with the self-contradictory effort involved in denying truth altogether, thus reappears in empiricism on a smaller scale: with the added inconsistency of positing dogmatically the multiple, consecutive, and well-known moments in which experience and "truths" are to be lodged.

The attempt to ignore the being of truth will be
discussed later: here I am concerned only with the
increment of physical reference requisite to
raise intuition into truth.   If spirit were not
incarnate, if it had no bodily organ, if in
consequence it were not domiciled in the
material and temporal world so that certain
things did not press upon it and trouble it
more than others, if in a word it had no
object but the realm of essence, then truth
would not need to enter into its thoughts.   For, in
that infinite field, no truth would be found distinguishable from the structure of pure Being, in which
every alternative is equally present.   Only if the spirit
became by chance self-conscious, and distinguished
its survey of essence from the field of essence itself,
and wondered why this survey should occur in this
particular order and have these arbitrary limits in scope
and direction—only then would truth, in its contingent
fatality, loom before the mind, truth and fatality
coming into being together with existence: because
evidently the spirit, with its intensity and insecurity
of attention, and its rambling progress, pre-eminently
exists.

In reviewing pure essences truth is involved not regarding essence but regarding the history of spirit.

Truth, in dialectic, is decidedly ironical and back-
handed.   What the reasoning mind demonstrates and
discovers is only a certain figure in the
tapestry of ideas.   This figure is, in that
realm of essence, interwoven with every
other possible figure, and is in no sense *the true*
figure proper to essential Being, because essential
Being, by definition, is infinite and contains all figures.
Yet the reasoning mind, in threading that particular
path in the labyrinth, is really exploring the truth
regarding the initial occasions and fundamental categories of its own thinking.   In chopping wood or in
using words men originally lighted upon the square

Biological freedom of dialectic.

and the triangle, and defined those essences. These essences are true of those blocks or of those conventional concepts and categories of speech; so that any further elaboration, by dialectic, of the essences chosen, is by implication true also of those blocks and those notions. At least it must be so if the original affirmation of the square and triangle was true absolutely: but it may well be that these ideas arrested by thought were only loosely applicable to the existing objects: in which case the more those ideas were elaborated dialectically, the further probably would they stray from the truth.

Existence, as if charged with electricity, turns a whole region of essence into a magnetic field. Not merely do the characters materially embodied in some fact or event become, as it were, incandescent, but all the still opaque essential relations of those characters become pertinent to that existence. A fertile mind will contrast the fact as it is with the fact as it might have been: especially as the movement of external events and the movement of intuition go on at different rates and in incongruous directions. Intuition, for instance, often runs backwards, as evolution cannot do; or jumps over space and time by confusion of similars; while nature endlessly repeats similars, but never identifies them, and never leaves out the alien context that separates them and renders them existentially many. The play of intuition over the realm of essence, though limited and guided by the genius of each psyche, is far freer than the plodding blind course of cosmic events. Imagination makes comparisons, conceives alternatives, regrets that they were not realized, ventures to prophesy their realization, becomes inspired, and ends perhaps by condemning the whole world, and calling it deceptive and false, in contrast to the shining "truth" of what it ought to be. All the errors, illusions, pathetic fallacies, and poetic myths with which the human mind disguises the truth are so many borrowings from outlying regions of essence; characters interpolated in lieu of characters undiscovered, or extensions of the characters actually found.

It is not always fancy, however, or religious passion, that flies from accidental truth to necessary possibilities: cold logic may do so also. Let a fact have any total character you choose: it will at once be true not only that this fact has this character, but that it has not any other character. But all the other characters, which this fact has not, compose the realm of essence in its residual infinity. If this fact be John Smith, it is true not only that he is John and Smith and man and mortal, but that he is *not* Jonah, *not* the whale, *not* Jehovah, *not* any other of the disparate things that infinite patience might enumerate. Thus, by privation and negatively, any fact drags the whole realm of essence into the realm of truth, or rather into that of error; since outlying essences are here introduced, not by genial intuition of their ideal being and sympathy with that variety of forms, but in a fault-finding and depreciatory tone, as things missing and false. It is in this way, perhaps, that a starved Puritan, clutching the bare bones of reality with a material terror, might conceive the realm of essence, and think it the abyss of night.

The impertinence of qualifying the outlying realm of essence as false may confirm the impropriety of qualifying it as true. False and true are nether accidents: and their very contingency renders it impossible for us to say to what extent they may, in the end, colour the realm of essence with truth or falsehood: for there is no knowing how much of essence, in the end, may be exemplified in existence, or may fail to be so exemplified. The congruous interest, in respect to essence, is logical and æsthetic,

All that is not truth becomes, for belief, the field of possible errors.

not documentary or moral. Or, rather, no interest, and no reference to events, is congruous at all, but only the infinite plasticity of intuition playing over the infinite variety of Being.

Before going deeper into this subject, it may be well to make explicit the sort and degree of validity proper to such an argument. Much less is being asked of the goodwill of the reader than he may at first suspect, and nothing at all is being asked of his credulity. I am not defending any belief. The only belief that I myself entertain, because I find it irresistible, is the belief in a realm of matter, the expectation of persistence and order in a natural world; and this is a belief which I am confident the reader shares, although he may prefer to express it in other words. It is only as details in an assumed natural world that the reader and the very book I am writing exist for me at all. But the realms of truth and of essence are in quite another case. To them I assign no existence; in them I demand no belief. They are not to be conceived as hypothetical regions of fact, annexed to the realm of matter, as heaven and hell might be annexed. The smile of the critic who will not be fooled into *believing* in them is entirely justified. They are not proposed as objects of belief. They are proposed as conceptual distinctions and categories of logic; as one of many languages in which the nature of things may be described. Anyone who wishes is free to discard these categories and employ others. The only question will be how he will get on; what sort of intellectual dominion and intellectual life he will achieve; also whether he will really be using other categories in his spontaneous and successful contacts with the world, or only a different jargon in his professional philosophy. Professional philosophies, sincere and even impassioned enough in controversy, are often but poor

(margin note:) Optional character of human logics.

hypocrisies in daily life. But the fortunes of other systems do not concern me. I am addressing those only who are willing, for the time being, to accept my language.

CHAPTER VI

CONVENTIONAL TRUTHS

SUPPOSE I open the newspaper and read: Sun rises 7.35 a.m., sets 3.58 p.m. Apart from some misprint or other casual error easily corrected, this information is undoubtedly true and accurate: it is supplied by the Greenwich Observatory. Good sense will prevent me from taking the statement absolutely or physically, and making it false. The sun of itself never rises or sets; and even in relation to human observers it seldom rises so late or sets so early: this, on the sun's part, is an extreme wintry laziness. The proposition is meant to be historical, not general or scientific; and like all historical propositions, describing incidental facts, it depends for its truth on its incidence: that is, on fixing the time and place to which it refers, as in this case to London on November 25th, 1935. Nor have we here a precise historical truth in psychological terms, telling us what was the experience of particular individuals at particular moments. Probably no Londoner saw the sun rise or set on that 25th of November: if truth were reduced to truths of experience there would be no truth at all in this matter. All that is meant is that, at that date, the astronomical conditions were such that, if there had been no clouds, no fog and no smoke, the first and last rays of the sun would have struck the London chimney-tops at those hours, or would have struck

Current information probably true, if taken as it is meant.

49

the eyes of any Cockney then looking in the requisite
direction from his attic window.

A certain and accurate truth may thus be conveyed
in conventional terms which in themselves are loose
and inaccurate.   Implications as to what has happened
physically, and hypotheses as to what might have
happened psychologically, may be placed before the
human mind by a figure of speech that will not bear
pressing, yet is unequivocal enough for human purposes.   Almost all the knowledge we have of nature
and of history visits our minds in this conventional
form, clothed in metaphors and idioms proper to our
grammar, and not seriously misleading our action or
expectation, though leaving us in ignorance or in
childish illusion about the proper texture of the
facts.

An animal vision of the universe is, in one sense,
never false: it is rooted in the nature of that animal,
Truth   aroused to consciousness by the circum-
claimed and   stances of the moment.   These circum-
actually
present in   stances, as well as that animal endowment,
all experi-   will therefore be expressed in the vision;
ence.   and when I say "expressed", I do not mean
passively betrayed by some quality or detail in this
vision, but, since consciousness is implied, I mean
noted, described, and known in some measure, and
in terms no matter how subjective.   In a word, the
vision claims to be true; and it possesses truth at least
in this fundamental respect, that it has a real object
and is not an idle mental phenomenon.   It is true
enough to be false, and to require correction.   For
the whole view of mind characteristic of modern
philosophy, that mind is a train of self-existing feelings
or ideas, is itself false.   Mind is spirit; a wakefulness
or attention or moral tension aroused in animals by
the stress of life: and the prerequisite to the appearance
of any feeling or idea is that the animal should be

alive and awake, attentive, that is, to what is happen-
ing, has happened, or is about to happen: so that it
belongs to the essence of discoverable existence, as a
contemporary philosophy has it, "to-be-in-the-world".
The observable details, the sounds, lights, darting
pains, curious somatic feelings, etc., are not separately
given to pure intuition, as they might be to a dis-
embodied spirit: they come in and from an imposed
and assumed world, an object of concern, alarm,
desire, or avid possession; and this material incubus
is felt and posited as an incubus, as air is felt and
posited in the struggle to breathe, not pictorially or
ideally, but as a besetting reality. Agony posits it,
and sensation or fancy afterwards study and describe
it, if they have the leisure. But the greater part of
life, and the deeper levels of it always, vaguely but
indomitably posit existence in a world; they speak for
a living organism floating or struggling in a foreign
medium. In positing such existence, and thereby
claiming some degree of truth, spirit exists and is
incarnate: and this primordial claim to truth is valid;
because in fact spirit lives only in animal organisms,
and these live only in a habitable world.

Having thus stretched, as it were, the canvas of
truth, or a real world to explore, the mind begins to
lay on such colours as its palette supplies. These
are mixed in the organs of sense; they are lighted up
by the passions; yet with this moral light and that
sensuous texture they are normally predicated of the
object, and used to define its nature: never its substantial nature, for that remains always the dynamic
counterpart of the action which arouses attention and
evokes faith; but the circumstantial nature of the
object, and the form it is to wear in human discourse.

Here are two stages of conceptual illusion, dressing
up conventionally the fundamental truth of human

E

knowledge. There is really a world, and there are real objects in each case to be described: but the images of sense used to describe those objects are not found there, but are created by the organs of sense in the observer: and the syntax of thought by which these appearances, which in themselves are pure essences, are turned into predicates of substance, is a mere expedient of human logic: so that while we gain true acquaintance with the real world, in that we distinguish its parts and their relations up to a certain point, we conceive these realities fantastically, making units of them on the human scale, and in human terms. Our ideas are accordingly only subjective signs, while we think them objective qualities; and the whole warp and woof of our knowledge is rhetorical while we think it physically existent and constitutive of the world.

Action, carrying belief with it, meets the reality, while sense and thought supply the poetic appearance.

The exuberance of nature stultifies and overwhelms any specific being that makes itself, or is made, the measure of all things; and the human mind in particular is doubly perplexed when it begins to discover on the one hand that things are not quite as they seem, and on the other hand that its own images and rhetoric are poetical. But an angry or despairing temper of criticism in either direction would be ill-considered. What is there wrong or paradoxical in the fact that the sensations and reactions of an animal must express directly his own nature, and only indirectly the nature of the forces affecting him? And what is there vain or scandalous in emotion, in original sensations, or in the poetic freedom of mind? Undoubtedly the essential potentialities of spirit are not exhausted by a specifically human experience; and intellect cannot help aspiring to omniscience, and to the knowledge of things as they are;

Animal knowledge must be limited in scope and biassed in quality.

and in practice, the conduct as well as the imagination of man stumbles and suffers rude shocks when vital presumptions are contradicted by events. There is accordingly something urgent about truth in our ideas, and something dangerous and ignominious in their falseness. But such urgency and danger touch not the inner rhetoric of thought, but only its practical symbolism, and the concomitant action. We must not be *misled* by imagination; there is no likelihood and no need that, in a miraculous sense, imagination should be clairvoyant.

All troubled and vehement scepticism, therefore, rests or ought to rest on economic considerations. The war against religion, the war against pictorial and logical thinking, is a commercial war. The poor, the hard-pressed, rebel against being taxed for such luxuries. They think mankind cannot afford to be human.

Recent science, both in physics and psychology, has responded, perhaps unwittingly, to this commercial interest. It is proud of not being deceived, and of wasting no energy on superfluous ideas. Physics can be reduced to pointer-readings, psychology to the statistics of behaviour. No doubt they can, for commercial purposes: and it may be convenient, in expert calculations, to abstract from all other considerations. But suppose we were willing to use only mathematical equations in conceiving matter and the dynamic connection of all events: the rest of our experienced or imagined world would then be explicitly transferred to another sphere, let us call it mind; and this variegated experience (not open to psychological science, which treats of behaviour only) would become enormously important and, except for the mechanical or medical expert, alone familiar. Even the expert would continue to

Commercial radicalism in philosophy retains only autobiographical truth.

live in the human world, using his science only in
occasional professional excursions beneath the surface
of phenomena: and his scientific conception of the
underlying forces or processes would be too tenuous
(unlike mythology) to draw away his instinctive belief
from the pictorial universe of the vulgar. His philosophy, if he stopped to frame one, would probably
be empirical and idealistic: he would regard his science
not as truer than appearances, but as an intellectual
fiction based upon them and somehow serving to
predict them. Only autobiography could be quite
true.

It is not, however, on the lines of autobiography
that mankind conceives the world. Not literary psych-

But physics
and even bio-
graphy, for
mankind,
remain pic-
torial.

ology but pictorial physics dominates the
conventional mind. When we walk abroad
absorbed in the landscape or in picturesque
episodes and street-scenes, a philosophical
critic might say that we were occupied with
our own sensations, and not with the truth of nature
or of society: but though this may be his analysis,
it is not our conviction. And even when we are
reading history, poetry, or novels, what probably fills
our minds is pictorial physics. Suppose I am thinking over the life of Napoleon. I make no attempt to
recover his unrecoverable stream of ideas. Instead,
I imagine his mother, his military college, his uni-
forms, his habits, his books, Toulon, and the Tuileries;
and I sprinkle over those material scenes a few reported
words of the hero. I imagine his life as I might have
watched it, not as, in his inner man, he may have
experienced it. Yet the scenes I evoke are, to some
extent, the very scenes he witnessed and acted in:
and I actually re-live a part of his experience in
recalling some of the objects that surrounded him.
Pictorial physics, or the human aspect of material
things, thus forms the principal element possibly

common to various minds; and we have no way of imagining other people's emotions save to imagine their predicaments.

A curious compensation results in regard to truth in fiction. Nothing that exists can escape from the purview of truth; and all fictions touch the truth at least in this point: that they have in their day a psychological existence, so that a true history of fictions is conceivable. Established fictions are standards for true intercourse. But conventional fictions touch the truth also in a technical way, which is more intimate. In the act of being repeated or communicated, they are named and defined. Their conventional essence becomes a standard essence in human discourse, which may be spoken of congruously or incongruously, truly or falsely, according to the accepted usage. And this is not merely a matter of language and social propriety: because when an essence is once clearly focussed and distinguished in the mind, exactness in reproducing it, or fidelity in expanding it, excites a pleasant feeling of recognition, and euphoria; whereas incompatible variants, passing under the same name, become offensive and, as we say, *false*. Obviously no essence is false to itself; but a violation of convention is false to the context and expectations woven about standard essences in the public mind, that is, in the private mind when socially controlled. There is a vital discord, and the incongruous note that produces it is called a false note.

The vital character of such discords and harmonies justifies a human trait which, at first sight, might seem scandalous to a moralist. Convention, correctness, orthodoxy are far more intimately precious to mankind than truth. The world of things seems arid and alien compared with the inexhaustible world of talk; and a man will laugh at his mistakes about matters of fact, Convention is naturally more human and beautiful than truth.

when shame will consume him all his life long if he
has slipped into a fault of speech or of manners.
Not merely, too, for social reasons, because other
people may be laughing at him. The inner beauties
of convention are glorious to develop, and its tissue
painful to rend. Need I mention music, rhetoric,
and social ritual? Perhaps the speculative part of
religion, pure myth or metaphysics or theology, will
show the power of convention best, because here the
inspiration is so potent that it overflows all barriers,
overcomes the judgment and claims positive truth for
its fictions. Not only in the maniac and the prophet:
often at second hand, when social countenance supplies
the lack of physical sanctions, and when types of
religion, as of language and manners, become things
to fight for and to be true to at the sacrifice of all
other interests, especially that of truth.

A philosopher who has discovered his principles
for himself may wear them with a good grace; but
Zeal for   one who has adopted them from other
tyrant ideas. people is likely to be a fanatic. Nothing
infuriates a man more than to be contradicted in the
convictions which he has learned with care, accepted
on high authority, and made the centre of all his
thoughts. Not only are his proud views thereby
cheated and mocked, but the fact that this precious
orthodoxy was after all acquired, and perhaps not
altogether persuasive at first to the inner man, doubles
the alarm. The scoffer outside is not without a silent
ally within; and the outrage is intolerable that the
same world that once taught us all these difficult
things and induced us to conform to them at a great
secret sacrifice of our inclinations, should now coolly
proceed to teach us something different, require us
to back our engines and to revise our affections,
already so artificially constrained and elaborately
stimulated. Our strait-jacket has grown into the

flesh, and we are ready to flay any man who would tear it from us. Not only do we regain our freedom with a sigh; we know too well that it will not be freedom but only slavery to a new convention, probably more external and repulsive to our inner nature than were the older traditions. For if those traditions were wrong, it was chiefly because they were too spontaneous, too boldly human and conceited; and anything contrary to them is likely to be doubly contrary to the heart.

All this usurpation of truth by convention is inevitable in a being as richly endowed psychically as man is, so that his inner life is ready to breed world upon world, while at the same time he is so hard pressed by matter and by society, that his imaginative fecundity is *The great deceiver of mankind is man.* continually cut short, and he is compelled instead to attend to the hard facts. Hence all the disappointments of spirit. We are condemned to live dramatically in a world that is not dramatic. Even our direct perceptions make units of objects that are not units; we see creation and destruction where there is only continuity. Memory and reflection repeat this pathetic fallacy, taking experience for their object, where in fact everything is sketchy, evanescent, and ambiguous. Memory and reflection select, recompose, complete and transform the past in the act of repainting it, interpolating miracles and insinuating motives that were never in the original experience but that seem now to clarify and explain it. This second fiction, mythical or intellectual, may serve in one way to penetrate beneath the veil of sense, and render us responsive in poetry and religious symbolism to the deeper currents of nature. Convention in such cases, while filling the imagination with fables and dramas, may really adjust human feelings and actions to the truth; and if mathematical science, in violent abstrac-

tion, traces the material movement of things with the
greatest accuracy attainable by mind, perhaps religion
and traditional precept may more poetically but more
voluminously respond to the same movement, in so
far as it affects human happiness.   Yet such harmony
between convention and reality is always imperfect;
and the hold that convention has on mankind is not
at all proportional to its rational justification.   The
tight opinionated present feels itself inevitably to be
the centre and judge of the universe; and the poor
human soul walks in a dream through the paradise of
truth, as a child might run blindly through a smiling
garden, hugging a paper flower.

CHAPTER VII

DRAMATIC TRUTH

THE dramatic moral climate in which our lives are passed is not other than the climate of matter but only a passionate experience of the same. Society does not present two separable worlds, one the world of men's bodies and another less earthly one, that of men's minds. A world of mere minds, a heaven with its legions of invisible and bodiless angels, if conceived at all, exacts no belief from the sceptic. I am as far as possible a sceptic, and a world of that sort does not figure in my philosophy. On the other hand, a world of mindless automata, like the *bêtes-machines* of Descartes, is a violently artificial object, conceived in purely mathematical and mechanical terms, although the terms in which that object is actually perceived are primarily sensuous and dramatic. The object is a body with the motions perceived or expected in that body; but these bodies do more than amuse the eye. Some are noxious or wild beasts; some are members of your own family. They suckle or hit you; and you know them apart by their works before you distinguish them clearly by their aspect. Even the most crudely physical forces wear a dramatic aspect when their action is violent, or for any reason arouses violent emotion. Spirit in us then rises or falls; and the cause is felt to be the action of spirits and gods: mythical beings not added fancifully to physical beings clearly conceived to be physical, but moral energies recognized

Moral dimensions found in the world are readings of matter in dramatic terms.

59

as the very core and secret of the material facts.   That
souls exist and that they move bodies is indeed the
primary form in which any sensitive soul will conceive
the forces of nature.

A soul, a dramatic centre of action and passion,
is utterly unlike what in modern philosophy we call
consciousness.   The soul causes the body

The actual
flux of events, to grow, to assume its ancestral shape, to
either in   develop all its ancestral instincts, to wake
nature or
conscious-   and to sleep by turns.   The soul determines
ness, is not what images shall arise in the mind and
dramatic.
what emotions, and at the same time determines the responses that the living body shall make
to the world.   Consciousness is only an inner light
kindled in the soul during these vicissitudes, a music,
strident or sweet, made by the friction of existence.
With this light and music, purified and enlarged, fancy
has peopled heaven; but on earth the course of consciousness is helplessly distracted: a miscellany of
conventional half-thoughts and evanescent images.
A sympathetic intuition of such actual consciousness
in another person often comes by imitation or by
unison in action.   When caught in a common predicament, we involuntarily understand one another.   Each
feels what everybody else is feeling; and the same
thing happens, less voluminously, in ordinary conversation.   Such mutual understanding is not in
itself dramatic, though the occasion of it may be so;
it is neighbourly, attentive, playful, as when we understand a child, a comrade, or an author.   Spirit is
essentially disinterested, even in tracing the fortunes
of spirit.   But when physical contagion ceases and
this brotherly spell is broken, we remain as profoundly
ignorant of the fountains of life in others as in ourselves.   The volatile spirit which was ours for a
moment is fled we know not where.   Hence in consecutive politics or economics the experts are quite

blind, lost in a labyrinth of facts not understood, and appalled at the insidious transformation of these avowed motives and ideas by which action was supposed to be guided.

Dramatic intuition, on the contrary, springs from the passions, that is to say, from the principles of action. A man may be conscious of his passion, in that he feels strangely agitated and is affected by everything in a strange way. But the passion itself is a force, a physical automatism let loose within him, and altogether other and deeper than his consciousness of it. If he attempts to put it into words, or to conceive its proper nature, he is driven to dramatic fictions in one sense more remote from actual passion than were his inarticulate feelings or hot words: he is driven to myth or to dialectic. In a fable, or in a logical trope, he imaginatively draws the outline and traces the movement of that mysterious influence which troubles him; and the truth facing his passion, as he is best able to conceive it, is a dramatic truth.

The dramatic sense depicts not consciousness elsewhere, but tropes affecting one's own passions.

Here all is expectation, partiality, superstition, hyperbole, rage, and enthusiasm. The accuracy possible in prosaic literary psychology is sacrificed to a summary eloquence. Yet not without compensation in the direction of truth. Dramatic genius can afford to be unfair to the surface facts, to foreshorten, crowd, and caricature everything. It is not interested in accompaniments, however real in themselves, which it finds irrelevant; it is not interested in justice; it is interested only in great issues, and in the secret tendencies that may be making for the ultimate triumph or defeat of one's own soul. If the facts are to be dramatized, they must not be reproduced. They must be recast selectively on a grand scale, and precipitated towards some climax in which the heart is concerned.

Yet if they are to be truly dramatic, these relations must not be invented. They must subsist in the realm of truth. Intuition simply comes to disengage them from what is morally irrelevant, and to trace the red vein of destiny running through the world.

Dramatic intuition, or apt myth, has many forms or stages, from animism to dialectic and wit, from superstition to natural law. These intellectual unities may be true of the world without being parts of it. Every trope discerned in nature, every self-repeating movement, assumes a vital unity in the mind. Whatever happens, when it elicits a living idea, seems to have happened with a purpose. This illusion is normal and even a sign of intellectual force, because the first phase of any trope, when that trope has once been noticed and has taken root in the psyche, comes essentially as merely the beginning of what ought to follow, and a sure omen of the total movement to come. So the first part of a sentence, especially in an inflected language, can hardly appear without prophetic reference to the remainder. In nature, however, any trope may be cut short. It is not a power, as intellectual superstition may fancy, but only a customary rhythm established contingently and subject to interference from every quarter, until it finally becomes unrecognizable or vanishes altogether. Yet so long as it subsists, it describes as well as is humanly possible a whole obscure region of nature from the point of view of some soul. Dramatic fiction may thus reveal to us the gist of existence, as flat experience and prosaic observation could never do.

That which lifts dramatic perception above mere poetry or fiction is its moral origin and its practical sanction. Taken for cool descriptions of the facts,

Mythical units may express important movements otherwise untraceable.

what would the myths of Freud be, or the dialectics of Hegel and Marx, except grotesque fancies? But there is method in this madness. Freud is an alienist, a healer of souls, Hegel fundamentally a theologian, Marx a revolutionary. Each studies a practical momentous problem, how to restore health and sanity, or justify a progressive worldly religion, or provoke and guide a social upheaval. They review the history of their moral problem in its own fantastic terms. They seek to understand and to govern passion by passion. In such treatment—for it is a treatment—the total cosmic truth must be denied or left in the shadow. Instead we have a sort of war-map in which nothing is set down but what touches the campaign of the season. Yet even so, the perspectives opened up may be infinite, since everything in the world touches everything else at a certain remove and at a certain angle; and we may be dramatically enlightened, in the service of our passions, whilst perhaps by these passions themselves we are being intellectually deceived.

The enormous infusion of error that sense, passion, and language bring with them into human knowledge is therefore less misleading than might be supposed. Knowledge is not truth, but a view or expression of the truth; a glimpse of it secured by some animal with special organs under special circumstances. A lover of paradox might say that to be partly wrong is a condition of being partly right; or more soberly, that to be partial is, for knowledge, a condition of existing at all. To be partial and also to be relative: so that all the sensuous colour and local perspective proper to human views, and all the moral bias pervading them, far from rendering knowledge impossible, supply instruments for exploration, divers sensitive centres and divers inks, whereby in divers ways the facts may be recorded.

Error itself a true index to its causes.

A radical instance of dramatic truth appears in sentimental time. ` Time is not *in truth* sentimental:

Dramatic element inherent in knowledge.
the past is not fading, the future is not empty or unreal; and when a man is moral and rational he recognizes the intrinsic reality and importance of both those regions, vitally so obscure and intangible.   Yet if he could be absolutely rational and moral, if his mind could possess impartially all the past and all the future, he would be dead, he would be deified, he would have become motionless and eternal like the truth itself.   The forward direction of his thought and the backward vista of his memory would be neutralized.   He would be omnipresent; and this intimate identity of his mind with all possible knowledge would make experience, in any tentative progressive sense, impossible for him. And unless he somehow removed himself from the whole reality of himself and held it at arm's length, even the eternal and complete truth of it would elude him: because he would be that totality, and could not survey it.   So the irrational finitude and bias of animal life, far from denying us the truth, summons us to pursue the truth, and gives us, in some measure, the means of attaining it.

I know how irritating constantly superstitious, rhetorical, moralistic views can be to the truth-lover;

Foolish effort to eliminate it.
yet we must give the devil his due, and consider the consequences of refusing to think humanly when we are human. Thought itself would have to be abandoned in favour of mechanical notation of details.   Such notation, in chronicles, statistics and pointer-readings, would not enter the realm of truth at all, if a certain selection and synthesis did not preside over the record: it would otherwise not be descriptive, as truth is, but merely a concomitant echo or mechanical index to certain features in the world; a part of the world, then, and

not a part of the truth about the world. To this, indeed, a certain positivistic and ultra-empirical philosophy professes to reduce science, replacing science in act, which is a category of spirit, with the instrumentalities or procedure of science, which lie in the realm of matter. Here, out of respect for the truth, we have an attempt on the part of mind to suppress mind; but although the truth is ontologically no more mental than physical, it is a form, an essence, that intelligence may find in an object, or in a system of objects, and by no means of part or member of that existential reality. Truth is therefore something that only mind can detach, something, as it were, addressed essentially to mind; although in the order of genesis it is the being of truth, the fact that facts exemplify essences and have relations, that makes it possible and appropriate that animals should develop minds: that is, should become aware not only of their organic processes expressed in blind feeling, but should become aware also of the causes or the objects of those feelings, and discover some part of the truth about them.

Truth is therefore not discoverable at all without some vital moral impulse prompting to survey it, and some rhetorical or grammatical faculty, synthesizing that survey and holding it up to attention in the form of a recognizable essence. Dramatic myth, however poetical it may be or merely analogous to the facts, in that at least it responds to the facts reflectively, has entered the arena of truth; it is more cognitive, more intelligent, and more useful than a mechanical record of those facts without any moral synthesis. I think it very doubtful whether, if religion and poetry should dry up altogether, mankind would be nearer the truth; or whether science would gain anything by correcting its philosophical pretensions, for instance the pretension to truth, in order to become merely the technology of the mechanical arts.

Affinity of mind to truth.

Certainly nothing would be gained intellectually: and if we condemned intelligence, as well as imagination, to ticking like a clock, if not to total silence, we might outrage human nature too deeply, and provoke a violent reaction. It is more prudent for the critic of illusion to consider the truth that myth may possess rather than to attempt to escape from myth altogether.

Sanity requires spirit to practise a certain duplicity, and continually to correct its necessary language by a no less necessary mental reservation. We live in this human scene as in a theatre, where an adult mind never loses itself so completely in the play as to forget that the play is a fiction; and he judges it, not for what it pretends to present, but for the stimulus and scope of the presentation. So in the whole verbal, sensuous, and moral medium through which we see the world we may learn not to see the world falsely but to see ourselves truly, and the world in its true relation to ourselves. With this proviso, all the humorous and picturesque aspects of experience may be restored to the world with dramatic truth. The near is truly near, when the station of the speaker is tacitly accepted as the point of reference. The good is truly good, the foreign truly foreign, if the absoluteness of the judgment is made relative to the judge. And this judge is no vagrant pure spirit. He is a man, an animal, a fragment of the material world; and he can no more annul or reverse his hereditary nature, in reference to which things are truly foreign or good, than he can annul the external forces playing upon his organism. Thus in reporting his passionate judgments, as if they were self-justified and obligatory, the dogmatist is unwittingly reporting a truth of natural history—namely, that at that juncture such judgments on his part are normal indexes to the state of the world, and not the least interesting element in it.

This dramatic medium is itself knowable and good.

CHAPTER VIII

MORAL TRUTH

MORAL ideas are usually hybrid. On the one hand, they may contain truth about matters of fact, such as that arsenic is poison, or that a man with more than the desired courage will be called rash, and with less, a coward. On the other hand, in recording these facts the moralist probably adopts and asserts in his own person the preference implied in those eulogistic or disparaging terms. He takes for granted that life is a good, that the approved degree of courage is a virtue, and that cowardice or rashness is a vice. He thus insinuates, as if self-evident, a moral judgment into his historical or psychological observations; and the possible truth of the latter may seem to him to support the truth of the former. But the nerve of moral judgment is preference: and preference is a feeling or an impulse to action which cannot be either false or true.

Confusion between ethical truth and moral preference.

It might conduce to clearness in this subject if we limited the term *morality* to actual allegiance in sentiment and action to this or that ideal of life; while the history of such allegiances, and of the circumstances and effects involved, would form a descriptive science to be called ethics or the science of manners. Truth in ethics would then be like truth in any other part of natural philosophy, and particularly rich and discoverable: because it would not require us to investigate the mysteries of physics or biology, but would accept

67

large material and historical facts on the human scale, would treat them as units, and would be satisfied with presenting them to the human conscience, to be judged *morally*. In this *moral* judgment, however, it is hard to see how there could be any truth. The only truth concerned would be that such a judgment was passed, that it was more or less general and lasting, and more or less passionate. But there would seem to be no conceivable object or reality in reference to which any type of morality could be called *true*.

Yet how many moralists or political philosophers are content with the support that physical facts and physical forces may lend to their maxims, and do not also claim a moral rightness for these maxims themselves? Such moral rightness in moral sentiment is either a tautology, meaning that what you prize you prize, and what you want you want, or it is a tangle of confusion. Any first moral reaction, perhaps of anger, can harden into a fierce absolute command. Any feeling, nursed and kept close in the dark, may fester into a categorical imperative. The imperative of life, the imperative of every unchecked impulse, is no doubt categorical; and a certain group of these impulses may easily become a code of duty or honour, traditional in some society, or in mankind at large. Utility or calculation or what Kant called heteronomy may have nothing to do with such maxims: they may be as spontaneous and free as laughter or love. But how should these automatisms be *true*? The word *true* in such a case is unmeaning, except perhaps as a vague term of praise, a mere reiteration of some automatic impulse, as if we cried Amen. Such repetition might seem harmless; yet verbal self-confirmation, coming to one's notions as it seems from nowhere or from above, tends to fanaticism. Language then becomes an accomplice and a sanction of the will: and from honest opposition

Fanatical abuse of the word true.

to our enemies in battle, we pass to envenomed refutation of their feelings as false. Each party hugs its maxims not as its own and worth being true to, but as the *only true* maxims. We might dismiss this as excusable heat and vapour, or as a technical solecism; yet when passion usurps the name of truth, the very idea of truth is tarnished and defiled.

Nevertheless, as usage leads us to speak of truth within the spheres of logic and of convention, so it leads us to speak of truth in morals. And there are good reasons for acquiescing in this extension of the range within which judgment may be called true or false. In willing as in knowing there is a good deal of substitution and representation. Moral passions, carried by words and ideas in themselves automatic, may be deceptive, may be hollow; they may pass like storm-clouds over the conscience, tragically misinterpreting the inmost and ultimate allegiance of the soul. Such passions, and the judgments they dictate, may be called false, since besides blinding us to many a matter of fact, they deceive us about our own fundamental needs and demands. Integrity, on the contrary, the clear allegiance of a transparent soul to its radical will, without being true to anything external, makes a man's choices true to himself. It banishes moral illusions. And the same true representation of latent interests may extend to political action; a government or a party may pursue true or false aims, in the sense of being or not being in line with the radical and permanent interests of the people. Thus truth and error may be possible in morals, in so far as they are truths or errors in self-knowledge.

Take, for example, the commandment: *Love thy neighbour as thyself.* Purely hortatory as this seems, it may be almost entirely translated into propositions that would be either true or false. In the sphere

A moral precept may be true or false in respect to moral interests in general.

of action—which if we distinguish moral from
spiritual life would also be the sphere of morals—
Ethical   an imperative is an order to a dependent,
matters   intended to be, by suggestion, a form of
of fact
are also   indirect or suspended compulsion. A
involved.   commandment to love would then be in
reality an order to act as if we loved, implying that if
we did not do so, our neighbours and God would act as
if they did not love us.   This would be a true or a false
prophecy, and it might guide the will as might any
other credible report about the field of action.   But
love, spiritually considered, is a feeling: and an imperative in the sphere of feeling becomes a little nebulous.
How should love be commanded?   It might perhaps
be awakened by contagion, in return for love—*amor che
a nullo amato amar perdona*.   Or it might be extended
from an object already loved to some kindred object.
Then, in terms of pure feeling, the precept might run
thus: Love thy neighbour, because God loves him; and
thou lovest God, because God loves thee.   Or less
emotionally: Value others for their own sake, because
they too are centres of life and of values.   Consider
them, as Kant counselled, always as ends and never
merely as means.   In fact and by nature they are ends
to themselves as much as you are an end to yourself.   Here, in respect to all living beings, and not
merely to other men, we reach a necessary truth,
since life means precisely the power in organisms
to grow and to propagate, as if they loved their own
being.

Yet this ethical truth is not, and cannot become,
a moral commandment.   The categorical nerve of
every imperative is vital, it expresses an actual movement of the will.   And evident as the truth may be
that life in every form has its intrinsic values, and
attributes radiating values to all felt events, it by no
means follows that these values are unanimous or

that life in one form can adopt, or morally ought to adopt, the interests of life in every other form. This would indeed be the death of all morality, not the perfection of it. The will of the storm, the will of Neptune or of Jupiter Tonans, cannot with self-knowledge be adopted by the struggling and trembling creature about to be destroyed. The will of the enemy cannot be incorporated into that of the soldier. The will of the tempter, the interests of a rival in love, the tastes of the vulgar, cannot be weighed in the balance against the constitutive will and radical virtue of one's own being. Reason may harmonize the impulses of a soul: it would not be reason but self-betrayal if it abdicated these impulses in a brotherly compromise with cobras, monkeys, idiots, sophists and villains. Against a threatening deity, there is always some protecting deity to be invoked, or some other side of the same deity; and licence may be freely allowed to beasts and barbarians to live in their own way in their own preserves, so long as they do not trespass upon ours. Moreover, there is a mystical insight proper to spirit within ourselves—spirit not being specifically human—that perceives the universal innocence of life in the midst of universal war: but this insight cannot impose on the psyche in which it arises ways contrary to her native ways: nor has impartial spirit any reason for wishing to do so. Life is a form of order, a great rhythmic self-responsive organization in parcels of matter: but it arises in a thousand places and takes a thousand forms. If reason or spirit or any mystic influence whatsoever attempted to impose on each living creature the contrary impulses of all the others, it would induce not universal harmony but universal death. It would solve the moral problem only by dissolving all goods, all arts, all species and all individuals.

But ethical truths cannot inspire or annul natural moral preferences.

Just because moral life is inwardly grounded, physical truths are the only guide that it will willingly

Moral sentiment invents ethical fables.

accept. A contrary purpose merely arouses hostility, but a contrary fact may inspire caution. I remember in childhood the warning of my nurse against swallowing cherry-stones. If I swallowed them, she said, a cherry-tree would grow out of my mouth. This is the principle on which moralists usually recommend their system of morality. The preacher is honestly actuated by an unexplained intense sentiment which he wishes to propagate; and in order to do so he invents circumstances of a startling nature calculated to justify that sentiment. But the method is dangerous. The images evoked under such stress of feeling are likely to be grotesque, like the traditional picture of hell-torments, or the atrocities imputed to an enemy in war; and even if by chance the invention were true, or the fraud never discovered, the sentiments thereby aroused in a half-moralized public would wholly lack the intensity and purity of those that originally animated the preacher. Where he was all moral enthusiasm or sinister superstition, his flock will be lazy, prudential, or prim. For that which creates morality is not facts, nor the consequences of facts, but human terror or desire feeling its way amid those facts and those consequences.

Suppose that instead of laughing at my nurse I had been horrified at my thoughtless sin and terrible

Such sentiment is inevitable.

danger in having swallowed a cherry-stone: then moral experience in me would certainly have become vivid. Sundry *ethical truths* would incidentally become unpleasantly clear, such as that a tree growing out of my mouth would be embarrassing, not to say fatal; or that other little boys lacking that ornament would probably jeer at me. From these ethical truths my mind would be expected to jump automatically to the *moral judgment* that annoyance, derision and especially death are absolute evils, which ought to be avoided. Life indeed involves the moral judgment that life is a good, since, while life lasts, the organism tends to maintain or to restore the continuity and harmony of its functions, defending itself with a blind concentrated fury against mutilation, disease and death. Even when in some tragic moment reflection turns against instinct and prefers physical death to life, not everything in life is judged to be evil; for at least this high condemnation or renunciation of life is regarded as a glorious victory and liberation for the spirit; and what is spirit but the quintessence of life here purified into tragic knowledge, into clear loyalty to what is felt to be best? It is therefore an ethical truth that moral judgments of some sort are inevitable in man. He cannot help having some radical preference. However sublimated this preference may be, it will express his vital feeling, the last cry of his animal nature, morally groundless. This cry may be absolutely sincere and true to the heart; but there is no meaning in saying that the preference so uttered is a truth in itself.

In strictness we might even say that every moral judgment is repugnant to the truth, and that if consciousness fundamentally gave voice to truth rather than to life, and to the animal partiality involved in life, moral sentiment would be impossible. The cry, *How beautiful!* or *How good!* may be sincere, and it may be applauded, but it is never true. If sincere such a cry is also never false, even if not re-echoed by the public conscience; because the public feeling that contradicts it can also never be true, but at best also sincere. Where sentiment is diffused and unanimous, if one person utters those exclamations, all the rest may no doubt murmur, *How true!* And indeed, to that

But if turned into a predicate of things dictates a falsehood.

extent, the judgment will then be *true morally*: that is, it will express the bias of human nature. That mercy is good or the sunset beautiful may be true dramatically and conventionally, for the soul and in the speech of a particular moral society: a society that need not retract its judgments if by chance some harder head or colder heart contradicts them; rather it will judge those contrary judgments to be wicked and blind. And so they will be in respect to the standards of that society. There would be no further meaning, only a greater shrillness, in insisting that they are blind and wicked in themselves. If for the emotional words *beautiful* and *good* we now substitute the analytic words *admired* and *welcome*, all moral contradiction disappears, the fog lifts, and we restore our moral intuitions to their legitimate field, the field of self-knowledge.

This Socratic self-knowledge is not scientific but expressive, not ethical but moral; and here if anywhere, in the discovery of what one ultimately wants and ultimately loves, *moral truth* might be found. This is no easy discovery; and we must be prepared for surprises in morals, no less than in physics, as investigation and analysis proceed. As the blue vault vanishes under the telescope, so moral conventions might dissolve in an enlightened conscience, and we might be abashed to perceive how disconcerting, how revolutionary, how ascetic the inmost oracle of the heart would prove, if only we had ears to hear it. Perhaps a premonition of this ultimate moral disillusion rendered Socrates so endlessly patient, diffident and ironical, so impossible to corrupt and so impossible to deceive.

I think, however, that there was one ethical illusion unextirpated even from the mind of Socrates (as also from that of Emerson); an illusion that warped the moral impartiality of his precepts and rendered him partisan and dogmatic in spite of his intention to be absolutely courteous and fair. He assumed that human nature was single and immutable, and the soul qualitatively identical in all men. The good that glimmered like buried gold in his own heart must lie also in the hearts of others, and only ignorance or sophistry could keep them from seeing it. But the roots of the good are alive; they are far more tentative and curiously entangled than verbal debate might indicate at Athens amid a bevy of rationalizing demagogues and sophists. Even in the individual, in whom actual preference has its only possible seat, ultimate sincerity presupposes a definite psyche, with assignable aspirations; and indeed some degree of definiteness any psyche must possess, else that psyche could not be the hereditary principle of organization in the body or of direction in the will. Yet this vital definiteness is not absolute. At each moment there is a limit, inwards, below which the psyche is not sensitive to variations in her own substance; and there is a margin outwards toward the infinite, beyond which what happens does not affect her specific life. Moreover, the most radical demands of the psyche are not immutable. Unfelt variations in her substance transform and undermine her desires. She is mortal; presently she will make no demands at all; and in the interval, from germination to birth and from childhood to old age, she successively develops and outgrows functions which are essentially temporary. In her origin she was a new equilibrium that changing circumstances had rendered possible; and her organism remains always potentially plastic and internal to the flux of nature at large.

> False assumption in dogmatic morals.

Hence the absence of a need or a passion in one phase of life cannot be taken for an argument that such a need or passion is false or wicked elsewhere. The contrary assumption is the root of much idle

censoriousness and injustice in moralists, who are
probably old men, and sapless even in youth, all
their zeal being about phrases and maxims
that run in their heads and desiccate the
rest of their spirit.   To reach moral truth,
which like all truth is eternal, we should
have to remember or foresee with absolute clearness the
aspirations of all souls at all moments; and confronting
these aspirations with their occasions, we should have
to measure their relative vanity and physical compatibility.   The question is not whether they happen
to be identical or harmonious with our own sentiments.
We are particular creatures at one point in space and
time: and the most contrary goods are beyond mutual
censure, if pursued at different times or by different
spirits.

*The prob-
lem for the
moral
imagination.*

    Moral dogmatism is an attempt to stretch moral
unity beyond the range of natural organization.
Spiritually it is a sinister thing, a sin against
spirit elsewhere.   Yet politically, and within
the living organism, animal or social, moral
dogmatism is morality itself; it is the effort
of that organism to maintain its health and
attain its perfection.   Hatred or contempt
for alien manners and ideas would be absurd in a
philosopher sure of his own ground; he would be
pleased by their zoological variety which like that of
animals in cages would not seriously endanger his
safety, freedom, or peace.   But social morality—and
all morality is deeply social—is necessarily divided
at home and threatened from abroad.   Invective and
propaganda are instruments in this animal warfare;
they are useful in maintaining discipline, in breaking
the enemy's spirit, and in capturing as many loose
ambient forces as possible to the support of your
particular regimen.   Liberals and Pacifists, who
imagine they represent morality in general, are the

*Yet
conscience,
being en-
lightened
will, is
indomitably
positive.*

first to announce the sure victory of their cause and
the annihilation for ever of all their enemies, that is, of
all moralities in particular. Yet morality in general,
as we see in truly emancipated circles, is no morality
at all. The root of morality is animal bias: and to
renounce that bias would be to renounce life. Even
the most general and tolerant of moral standards—
harmony—is not a good in itself. There must be an
actual will directed upon harmony in order to render
harmony a good. Harmony demands many a sacrifice:
in what direction, and at whose cost, shall those
sacrifices be made? A strong and well-knit nature,
brave with the perfect harmony within, will despise
and detest harmony on a larger scale; it will refuse to
sacrifice any part of its chosen good, and will declare
eternal war on the devil, and on all his obsequious and
insidious agents.

Such, in whatever interest and on whatever scale,
is the nerve of morality. Reflected in the living soul,
all the rays of nature instantly acquire a moral colour.
Nothing can happen that will not be good or bad in a
thousand directions. When all living souls are considered, the cross-lights and conflicts of these values
spread an impenetrable tangle, through which it is
impossible for mortal eye to see the ultimate balance
of benefit and injury. But nature laughs at this
perplexity. A man is a man, for all the apes and
donkeys in the world. Instinct reasserts its primacy;
the overwhelming immediacy of some great passion
or hope breaks through the cobwebs of sentimental
idleness, and sets a fresh clear work before us that will
not brook delay.

This self-assertion is not always young and im-
pulsive; it may survive all experience and disillusion,
growing firmer in isolation, and cleaving to the chosen
good even when this is known to be unrealizable.
Such desperate heroism is nevertheless contrary to

all the lower unconsecrated yielding parts of the psyche; and half the martyr's mind, together with the mind of posterity, will judge wholly un-

Its ultimate deliverance is moral truth. realizable desires to have been unhealthy and undesirable. Moral truth, therefore, even at its purest, by no means bestows moral authority over alien lives. It signifies only complete, enlightened, ultimate sincerity.

CHAPTER IX

TRUTH SUPERTEMPORAL

THE relation of truth to time might seem simple enough if stated in general terms. Make a complete report of all events occurring in time and there you have the truth. But a complete report, though suggested and even in one sense pursued in all truth-telling, remains always a pure ideal. Be it in the witness-box or be it in the laboratory, that "whole truth" which we are pledged to tell can never be told. It would take too long, much longer than the events had taken to happen; and our means of observation are limited, as well as our means of expression. Moreover, when we enlarge the canvas and consider the total truth of the universe, we perceive that the impossibility of actually knowing it is intrinsic. In order that even a superhuman survey of history should be complete, the last of future events would have had to occur and to show its colours. Therefore an actual survey (which would be a fresh event) could not supervene; or if it supervened it could not be all-inclusive, since by arising, this survey itself would have added an important event to history.

The truth, then, forms an ideal realm of being impersonal and super-existential. Though everything in the panorama of history be temporal, the panorama itself is dateless: for evidently the sum and system of events cannot be one of them. It cannot

79

occur after anything else or before anything else.
Thus the truth about existence differs altogether in
ontological quality from existence itself. Life and
motion are gone, all scales are equally real, all ages
equally present. Intensity, actuality, suffering have
become historical. The truth is like the moon,
beautiful but dead. On the other hand, the truth is
much richer than existence can be at any moment.
Not only does it retain the essence of all moments
equally, but it contains much that each moment, and
even all moments in their inner being, can never
contain, since it contains also the systems which these
moments form unawares, merely by co-existing and
alternating as they do. Truth might be figuratively
called the memory of the universe; but it is far more
than that, since the destiny of the universe is included
in the truth. If we fancifully give the name of memory
to the past of the world, we must imagine that memory
to be complete and unmixed with error, else it would
not contain but contradict the truth of the past; whilst
in regard to the future, the truth would still loom
before advancing events with a tragic ambiguity, like
an oracle heard and known to the infallible, but as yet
impossible to decipher. Thus though the truth is
created by contingent events, and secondary to them,
and though destiny is but the confluence of successive
spontaneities, truth nevertheless confronts existence
with a divine authority and an insoluble problem of
self-knowledge. Nor is it congruous with the nature
of life that the truth should be completely revealed to
it. Glimpses come only in tragic moments or to
strangely disinterested minds; and the revelation is
dangerous, even when it seems entrancing. The
world at one moment, like Narcissus, may fall in love
with its own image, seen in the truth; but at another
moment that image may become a Gorgon and may
petrify the eye that beholds it.

The truth would not be complete if it left unrecorded that asymmetrical lapse and precipitation of motion in which it cannot participate. In the Change, translated into terms of truth, becomes the genealogy and measure of change. Events become the subject-matter of science and history. Constitutional incapacity to change is not a defect on the part of the truth, but on the contrary a proof of its staunchness and its privilege of permeating existence without forfeiting its own ideality. One event cannot be the truth of another. While each fact undergoes change by yielding up its place and substance to a new fact, the truth of that occurrence can be only the *form* of the successive facts with the *form* of the transition between them.

In the realm of truth events compose perspectives.

We should doubtless have no notion of change if we did not undergo it; yet it is not by merely passing that facts breed memory or an intuition of time stretching forward and back. It is the enrichment, the complexity, the multiform tensions of organic life as it flows that enable us to feel life flowing. Intellectual synthesis does not require any existential element to be in two moments at once; but material energies, rich in vital potentialities, can become conscious of changes on foot. This actually happens when a psyche, organized for growth and sensitive to opportunity, being adjusted both to the past and to the future, feels at each moment the suspense, duration and lapse of time. The canvas is then spread for imagination to paint upon, and history and science do nothing but fill it in. At each moment we are then accompanied by a sense of prolonged events in their wholeness, that is to say, as they lie in the realm of truth. For it is only in the realm of truth that events can be unified or divided. The very concentration of existence in the moving present

Change is revealed not by change itself but by complex tensions within each moment.

prevents any contrasts, repetitions, or derivations from actually disrupting that momentary reality; yet this reality, by continually pulsing and changing, renders such contrasts, repetitions and derivations true.

It is precisely this continuity of events and these truths about them that intelligence comes to perceive:

The reality of truth makes intelligence possible logically and supports it biologically.

not imagining and positing those truths falsely (as the enemies of intelligence would like to suggest) but imagining and positing them truly: because if there were no substantial derivation of event from event, and if generation were not bridged by the truth of generation, no proposition could have an existing object, and all signs and beliefs would be equally vain. For example: there could then be no identity between the child of A and the father of C, since B would be contiguous with each only under a different aspect; nor could the B who had A for his father be identical with the B whom A had for his son. In other words, each flash of change would be a separate universe; and events would therefore have no dates and compose no history.

Such a disruption of nature, or chaos of particulars, is not logically impossible. *It might be the truth*; but in that case all sensation and thought would terminate upon mere essence, and the idea of a flux of experience would be a false idea, since between actual moments there would be no transition, and time would be unrolled into a firmament of simultaneous facts. If chronology can be a true science, memory and dramatic imagination must be organs of truth; they must be truly inspired. The prophets of mutation, who say that all is change, are, against their will, shining instances of intelligence. Far from sinking with every wave, they keep their heads always above water, proclaiming how perpetually and pervasively the ocean flows.

It might seem, for instance, that the truth changes as fast as the facts which it describes.   On a day before the Ides of March it was true that Julius Cæsar was alive: on the day after that Ides of March it had *become true* that he was dead.   A mind that would keep up with the truth must therefore be as nimble as the flux of existence.   It must be a newspaper mind.

This, on the surface, is an innocent sophism, if not a bit of satire, mocking the inconstancy of things. Idiomatically we might as properly say, "It was then true that Cæsar was living," as we might say, "The truth is that Cæsar was then living."   In using the former phrase we have no thought of denying the latter.   If Julius Cæsar was alive at a certain

Verbal equi-vocation in transferring the tenses of affirmations to the truths affirmed.

date, it was then true, it had been true before, and it will be true always that at that date he was or would be or had been alive.   These three assertions, in their deliverance, are identical; and in order to be identical in their deliverance, they have to be different in form, because the report is made in each case from a different point in time, so that the temporal perspectives of the same fact, Cæsar's death on the Ides of March, require different tenses of the verb.   This is a proof of instab-ility in knowledge in contrast to the fixity of truth. For the whispered oracle, *Beware the Ides of March*, the tragic event was future; for the Senators crowding round Pompey's statue it was present; for the historian it is past: and the truth of these several perspectives, each from its own point of origin, is a part of the eternal truth about that event.

Beneath the surface, however, there is no doubt a remnant of metaphysical illusion, by which we transfer to physical time the sentimental colour of our tem-poral perspectives.   Instead of the physical truth that all men live in their own day and in their own day only, we say "Cæsar lived long ago"; or we may

G

even cry pathetically, "Cæsar is dead, long dead."
We thus slide from a truism to a private perspective,
and from a private perspective to a dramatic equivocation. For that Cæsar lived
long ago is true only in relation to our
own times; and that he is *dead, long dead,*
is not true of him at all, if we mean his life
or his consciousness, but at most might be
true of his corpse, if that still existed. But words lead
us to imagine that things can survive themselves. When
Cæsar has ceased to live, we half believe that he continues to exist dead. But nothing exists dead except
dead bodies. Facts exist only as they occur, and the
essence and truth of them, which are indeed eternal,
are non-existent. Names, however, being hereditary,
and essences being often exemplified repeatedly or
continuously in existence, we tend to attribute the
identity proper to the essence or the name to the
similar but diffused moments that inherit that name
or that essence. But between moments or facts,
however similar to one another, there is no identity.
The existence of each is internal and self-centred;
and each constitutes a primary contingent factor in a
world which, as a whole and in its detail, is perfectly
contingent and unnecessary. There is therefore metaphysical illusion or idolatry in peopling the world with
hypostatic identities and materialized truths: a curious
consequence being that truth and essence themselves
come to be obscured by confusion with the flux of
facts.

Two words in particular are apt to suffer this
hypostatis when truth is spoken of as changing: the
word *now* and the word *I*. I could once say truly: I
am now young. At present I can say truly: I am
now old. Therefore it would seem that the truth
about me is changed. But it was never true that I
am *now* young, if *now* means the year 1936; the *now*

Sentimental illusion in attributing temporal perspectives to physical time.

of fifty years earlier, though it had the same essence of actuality and was being lived through as breathlessly as the *now* of to-day, was an entirely different moment. And of that concrete moment it could never become true for me to say, Now I am old. The essence of nowness runs like fire along the fuse of time, but the particular spark is different at each point. The various contents of these various *nows* therefore combine perfectly to form the unchangeable truth of history.

The intuitive *now*, which is an essence, confused with the particular *nows*, which are facts.

Even deeper is the metaphysical illusion in hypostatizing the word *I*. Much used to be written concerning personal identity and responsibility: the soul in future had somehow to deserve damnation for its past sins, or for those of Adam. This moral enigma seems to have ceased from troubling, as if people were content to blame each moment for its own

And the transcendental *I* confused with the changing person.

folly; but the cognitive problem of memory still perplexes philosophers. Each man uses the word *I* to designate his physical person at all ages, awake or asleep: and the continuity of his body, bearing always the same name, leads him to think of himself as a self-identical being entering into relation with changing things. Yet his body (not to speak of his thoughts) notoriously changes faster than many a tree or river; whilst that in him which bridges time—pictured time only—is not a substantial fact at all but an intellectual faculty called intuition; and the occasions on which this faculty is exercised are themselves movements of the psyche, as transitory and irrevocable as any other events in nature. We may indeed give to all instances of intuition or feeling the common name of spirit, and may say that this spirit is identical at all moments and even in all persons; but such identity is qualitative only. Spirit in all those instances has the same transcendental status and infinite potential scope; it is everywhere intelligence in act; but this pure spirit or gift of consciousness flashes out only on scattered occasions. It is nothing substantial or permanent or continuous, capable by its prolonged existence of being present at once at every point of time. Such persistence is found only in objects on the human scale, that may be handed down like heirlooms, and still be conventionally identical; yet accurate physics dissolves even that prolonged identity into something formal and imputed; while in extending that analogy to spirit language goes wholly astray. Spirit being the flower of life is intrinsically fresh and self-positing at every moment; there is nothing identical in these moments except their spiritual essence. This essence the word *I* may indicate by its purely grammatical and generic force, when it stands only for the transcendental function of thinking, identical in all thoughts; but these thoughts or instances of thinking, far from being thereby materialized into a continuous fact, become each a transcendental centre for an ideal survey of time. They are lodged in physical time only by virtue of their organs. They are *intrinsically* dateless, as any synthesis of time must be in respect to the events it surveys.

Thus language may lead us to attribute to facts the timelessness of essences, and to create contradictions in knowledge where there is mere instability in existence. It is only when we ignore our own mutation that the truth seems to us to change.

CHAPTER X

COGNITION OF THE FUTURE

In human life it seems a matter of course to have much knowledge of the past and little of the future. This circumstance is exaggerated by some philosophers into a theory that the past exists now, and that the future is as yet nothing. Common sense hardly goes so far. The past, considered sentimentally as past feelings and adventures, seems rapidly to evaporate and grow ghostly as fresh events crowd upon the scene; while on the other hand all human prudence assumes a future to which the lessons of the past will apply. In mechanics and astronomy, exact predictions are constantly verified; and so, more loosely, is the great volume of daily expectations in human affairs. A cataclysm, perhaps, may intervene; but we feel that this too might have been foreseen had we been wise enough. In any case, there was a future to be known; and if human knowledge in that direction is so largely nebulous, while it is so rich and definite in respect of the past, the cause is to be found in a biological accident. This accident is that man is born helpless and passive, and must shape his instincts under the blows of experience.

The first experience of the human child is to be awake but helpless. He must tentatively acquire the art of walking, talking, and doing every other customary thing; things for which he is imperfectly ready, and which often cross his natural will, so that he is inclined

Knowledge of the past a human peculiarity.

to sulk and to attempt the impossible.   Hence a double
scar of defeat and compulsion marks all his progress.
He must skirt again the fatal vices of his ancestors,
and half his virtues have to be imposed upon him
as duties.   Therefore when opportunity smiles upon
him at last, he seldom can leap to meet it without
embarrassment.   His awakened instinct hesitates and
needs to be redirected by a revival of all the jolts
and disappointments and violent jibbings amidst which
it was formed.   He will recall his schooling in doing
what he has learned to do, and in his triumphs he
will still be redigesting his bitter failures.   No such
visionary memories need have accompanied his action,
had the lessons of the past become automatic in the
organism.   Any ghostly survival of the past would
then have signified some impediment or maladjust-
ment in the readiness to live.   But circumstances
alter natures; and in fact the only possible path for
man now runs round the loop of discipline and art,
and these circumlocutions have become integral to
the sort of perfection natural to him.   What he does
seems to him nothing, if he cannot remember what he
has done; and he would hardly care to live if he could
not conceive his background and his limits in living.

Consider, by way of contrast, the triumph of reproduction often approached in nature, when an animal
Instinctive   is born perfect.   In the womb or in the
attention   egg, where all his organs were preformed,
looks for-
ward rather   so as to be, in the ripeness of time, un-
than back.   erring in their action, he would have seen
no visions.   Such feelings as he may then have had
would never have been recalled or distinguished in
reflection.   His first daylight perception might well
be that of some lure or some challenge; and his whole
organism would instantly fly and meet it.   Perspectives
would all open towards the future.   The past, for
his consciousness, would remain an empty night and

an abyss of nothingness. His astonishment would be equal to his contempt, if he could hear that there were creatures called men, who thought that the future was uncertain, who expected to die, and whose mind was hung round like a mausoleum with skeletons and funeral inscriptions of things non-existent, which they called the past. The life of such a perfect animal, addressed altogether to the future, would be ruled by Passion and Duty, or perhaps it would be more accurate to say, by Honour. He would have an absolute vision of what *must* be done. Circumstances would never contaminate his will, but only call it forth, or defeat it; and the notion of a change of heart, or acceptance of anything short of the one perfect and absolute good, would seem to him the lowest depth of baseness.

I may seem to be writing a fable: yet the deeper parts of the human psyche are formed before birth. All our organs grow and preserve them- Biological selves without memory or experience, yet grounds of with remarkable adaptation to the future, foresight. that is, with biological foresight; and if these organs had a separate consciousness they would be in the same case as a new-fledged insect or a hungry beast. External influences would merely liberate internal powers. Even our outer organs of sense are in this case, since sights and sounds are, in their æsthetic quality, products of the eye and ear; yet their significant side for our lives is not this, but rather the indications they give regarding material facts existing outside at the moment. Suppose that instead of the eye or ear, which are comparatively passive instruments willing to be at rest, the organ were an empty stomach or a ripe sexual apparatus; the feelings involved would be turned, as sounds and colours are turned, upon the forces arousing them, but not as on static objects: rather as on objects of the chase, things to be caught or killed or eaten or possessed. However dumbly

and excitedly, it would be a vista towards the future
that would absorb the mind; and the intense attention
riveted on the present would contain a sensation of
imminent action, of something coming, that must and
that shall come.

Be it observed that the premonitory knowledge of
the future that I speak of is nothing miraculous; no
It is not *perception* of something by hypothesis not
perception acting upon the organs of sense. Perception
of the future. is definable as a sensation turned into knowledge of its ground, that is, of its present occasion.
A future occasion can therefore never be known by
perception. But it may be known by premonition,
by a rehearsal, as in a dream, of the acts to be per-
formed or the visions to be seen later. Evidently an
animal governed by instinct alone and incapable of
learning anything by experience, would be apt to have
such prophetic premonitions. Doubtless they would
not contain graphic images, until these were supplied
by perception; yet almost any hint will do to launch
an innate passion: as children at play in a barnyard
will feel the full thrill of standing on mountain-tops
or of cutting off heads. The self is as much alive
in sport as in battle, and less distracted; and the sheer
joy of achievement is never purer than when no
reasons or consequences are thought of.

Instinctive life is therefore quite competent to
anticipate the moral texture of the future possible to
Yet cognitive each creature; but that is not all. Premoni-
in function tions are more than anticipations; being
and carried by a definite impulse to action they
addressed are instances of animal faith, and fulfil a
to the requirement essential to knowledge of fact,
eventual
fact. in that they are beliefs positing a removed
object. Such premonitions can be true, because they
are assertions regarding the real future.

Moreover, occasions such as might provoke the

expected feelings are almost sure to occur, so that the premonitions are not only capable of being true, but are likely to be so. By hypothesis, *That to* the prophetic organism is perfect: but a *which* perfect and incorrigible organization would *instinct is* soon prove fatal unless it were well adapted *likely to* to the normal environment. We should not *come true.* be born with lungs if there were no air: and the promise of any instinct, when interpreted realistically, may be trusted, on the average, not to deceive us.

When natural prophecy fails, the failure eliminates the prophet in that particular instance, but it leaves prophecy alive and likely to be verified in *Instinctive* the experience of the race. Refutation by *prophecy* the facts can never abolish prophetic vision *incidental* until the organ of prophecy is destroyed. *failures.*

Being inwardly inspired, direct knowledge of the future can be only moral and dramatic, and limited to the future experience of the prophet or *It regards* of the people for whom he speaks. Such *only moral* fore-knowledge cannot extend to the date or *issues.* accidental circumstances of its fulfilment, nor to any cosmic facts beyond the range of the self-anticipating life.

Alleged *perceptions* of the future, as if by telepathy, may be admitted, when they seem to exist, but need not be explained superstitiously. They can *And is* hardly be direct intuitions of future events, *physically* seeing that no fact, either past or present, *conditioned.* is internal to intuition, or given as it occurs in its own medium; and as for the essence which intuition may actually evoke, it may as easily be exemplified in some future fact as in a fact that is past or contemporary. Prophecy may therefore be true conventionally, by anticipating an appearance in human terms, just as memory and perception are true conventionally, by supplying or repeating such an appearance. There is no telepathy in time or even in space, taken literally, as if essences flashed themselves about without other agencies; but the psyche in two removed persons may generate the same or partly the same images, through agencies not well known to us.

To be rational, to rely on memory and experience, to study and measure the movement of external things, Priority of will or instinct over memory even in man. is that great characteristic of man which has enabled him to construct instruments and to dominate the earth by his science and art. Nevertheless, even in man, this rationality and this accumulated knowledge of the past are something secondary. He is instinctive before he is rational, natural before he is artificial; and we may go further and say that he must look to the future before he can see the past. Memory is a mystery that psychology, as far as I know, has done nothing to penetrate. If it were the literal survival of the past, it would place us in the past, which we should think present, as in a dream; and the sense of pastness would not arise. If it were the revival of a specious past in the present, at a felt remove, with a temporal perspective of antecedent behind antecedent, the imagination would indeed be, so to speak, prophetic backwards; but whence, in that case, the suggestion of a real past with which our memory might be compared, a past which was the intended object of memory, and rendered that memory false or true? No doubt in the field of consciousness at any natural moment there is a sense of duration and lapse, as there is perception of motion; and both motion and lapse, studied analytically, involve a past given as past; or rather a specific part of the present over which a cloud of pastness, more or less transparent, rapidly spreads. If later the cloud seems to break in places, and show us again a bit of what once we saw, the identity of that past datum with our present datum becomes problematical: we may feel that our fresh intuition (in date, extent and relations manifestly a new intuition) is true as far as it goes, and that we remember the past exactly as it was; but this may be an illusion, inevitable in the absence of any possible fresh control of our recollection by the past occasion itself. The past, then, as far as direct memory and remembered experience can exhibit it, is like the future, a hypothesis in the air, since there is no evidence of the existence of its object except the hypothesis itself, and no possible test of the truth of this hypothesis, except that the compulsion to make it is irresistible.

Even that reflective life, therefore, on which man prides himself would be impossible if the impulse that creates prophecy had died out. The human assurance that there is a past rests on the organic assumption that there is a future. In memory the irresistible impulse to posit a world of action is turned backwards towards a world of origins: a useless and inappropriate turn in itself, because an idea of the past is a mere drag on life, except in the form of poetic legends rich in moral colour; and in that form the idea of the past is not true historically. It is not for its own sake that the past is worth knowing. Consciousness is essentially watchfulness, expectation, anxiety. Sleep would be sweeter; yet the well-fed senses are eager for exercise; or perhaps something foreign horribly invades our peace, and must be shaken off. In a word, Will lies beneath Idea. If the prophetic exercise of mind ever gives place to science, or dramatic to historical truth, it is only because Will has been defeated or intercepted by accidents which we have no means of removing, but may circumvent by some roundabout approach. It then becomes interesting to us to consider what those alien things are in themselves, how they behave on their own initiative, and by what artifice we may so far yield to them as, on the whole, to profit by

Faith and fear inherent in knowledge.

their existence.   We rehearse the past, but we rehearse it forward, as it moved when it was present; and even when we plunge backwards in imagination into antiquity, we do so as on a journey of discovery, unearthing one stratum after another, and letting buried truth tempt us on into the depths of its treasure-house.

So much for pointing out that life and mind posit the future initially, and that the same assumption *The truth of* animates not only each revival of the past in *the future is* memory, but even the belief in the pastness *independent* of the events recalled.   The past waits to *of any animal* *faculty to* be rediscovered as the future waits to be *conceive it.* fulfilled.   This initial assumption is imposed on us by life, and nature makes it dumbly in all her preparations; yet logically the reality of a future is not thereby proved.   Existence might collapse at any moment, spirit might vanish; and the truth of history, rounded out to that conclusion, might involve the truth that no time and no events existed beyond. Since existence is essentially contingent, the events composing physical time may be as easily finite as infinite, chaotic as regular; and their course is at liberty, as far as logic goes, to come or not to come to an end. Only visionary, synthetic, geometrical time is necessarily endless and steady.

That the future, if there is a future, will be what it will be, is an identical proposition, and necessary. *The future* That this pure tautology should have been *determinate* a cause of anguish to thousands of men, *even if not* *predeter-* desperately seeking refuge from it in a *mined.* thousand confusions, has, I think, a double source: partly in the trick of fancy that identifies vital freedom with chance, and partly in the trick of language that identifies truth with the knowledge of truth.   The truth of the future, like all truth, is eternal, and exactly as definite and complete as what, at any date, is the truth of the past: indeed, it is exactly the same truth, touching what is future from here and past from there. Facts cannot be indistinct or ambiguous in themselves. Suggested facts may exist or may not exist; but if *they* exist, they do so by having the precise character which they have. There is therefore no difficulty placed in the way of knowing the future by any inconsistence or indeterminateness in what the future will contain when it becomes present. The difficulties all come from blankness or want of range in the imagination of the prophet, or from want of affinity between his imagination and the forces by which the future will be really produced. A creature without memory cannot discover the past; one without expectation cannot conceive a future ; one without pre-adaptation cannot conceive the future truly. A creature having only momentary sensations, never fled from or pursued, would know absolutely nothing of the truth of things, since those momentary sensations would reveal essences evoked, not objects encountered, and the very notion of a world or of the truth about it would not arise.

On the other hand, the most intelligent and prophetic mind would be at a loss to predict anything truly, if events in the world had little kinship to one another, jumped into existence underived, and were spanned by no tropes on the scale of the images peopling that mind; for in that case impulses would be perpetually disappointed and calculations foiled. But this impossibility of predicting the future would not arise from any contradiction in that future, nor any ambiguity or incompleteness in the truth about it. It would arise from the accidental absence of tightness and regularity in the world to be discovered. In such a world inferential or intuitive knowledge of the past would be no less impossible than knowledge of the future. We might yield to the social persuasiveness of hearsay or legend; but we should be condemned to renounce all science in retrospect as well as in prophecy.

CHAPTER XI

TRUTH AND CHANCE

SPONTANEOUS oracles and prophecies which had much currency amongst the ancients have now fallen into disrepute. Life having become mechanical, anticipation has become so too. We construct artificial instruments accurately designed for their future uses, and we collect masses of statistics: yet it is extraordinary how blank our imagination is in regard to those events for the sake of which all our measures are taken. Our hands fashion the future, while our heads are full of the past. No harm ensues when the method of action is well established. A half-blind old woman may go on knitting usefully while she babbles old nonsense and vain regrets. Agriculture and trade may continue to prosper, while rival politicians take turns at the government. But in politics the most experienced men are the worst prophets, and the history of parties is a history of blunders. Here and there a genuine Hebrew prophet, like Marx, may divine and seem to direct the future, precisely in those large dramatic turns which the soul is ready for and foresees: the war of classes, which is always latent, may be stimulated into a paroxysm of mutual hatred, until only one class survives. Yet even when such is the genuine promise of the soul, machinery soon intervenes, and the course of events deviates into the unforeseen and the undesired.

Decay and revivals of prophecy.

When prophecy is trusted, the vital springs of prophecy necessarily feed history also, and the general theory of nature. For if oracular intuition, Classic summary and morally weighted, can predict theory of the future, it will thereby discover the prin- principles ciples that have governed the past also. with inci- The whole universe in that case must have occurring by a moral skeleton, such as intuition can "chance". divine. Yet as this moral skeleton is far from specifying the vast detail of events, two levels of truth come to be distinguished: fundamental, generic, universal truths, such as prophets may discern; and homely, accidental truths such as every man daily comes upon. This was the classic view of the universe. Platonic ideas, the genera and species of Aristotle, the axioms of logic, the geometry of bodies, the Ten Commandments, and the decrees of Providence determined the general nature of things and their ultimate destiny: and these were called "eternal truths". But the weather and the fortune of individuals were left to "chance". The tile dropping from the roof on the passer-by had for its intelligible "nature" or function to be a part of that roof, and not to fall from it; if it fell, it fell only by "chance". And the man, going about his normal business, passed by at that moment only by "chance". These accidental conjunctions did not express the true "nature" of anything: they occurred only because different "natures" or principles sometimes collided in the same matter, so that the event was hybrid and abnormal; or, more fundamentally, "chance" appeared in the passive resistance or sluggishness of matter everywhere, blotching the execution of every ideal design.

Truth, in such a system of moralistic physics, could acquire a meaning quite different from that which I assign to the word. Instead of being descriptive of existence, the truth would be a model for

existence: it would exhibit the world purified, trans-
figured, reduced to its essential principles.   The truth
would then paint an inspired, a flattered,
and therefore in my sense a thoroughly
false picture of reality.   Yet reality, for a
prophet, demands and justifies this neglect
of what exists only by "chance"; and the
bolder idealists will ultimately deny that
the accidents and evils and appearances
that seem to obscure that prophetic vision have
any reality at all: for having no *raison d'être*, no inner
justification for their momentary apparition, they are
illusions.   They collapse and annul themselves when
questioned, and are simply false.   The word truth
thus becomes a eulogistic term, as the word reality
does also.   Reality will exclude, not include, appearance; and truth will not be the eternal image of all
facts and illusions whatsoever, in the order of their
existence, but rather an *explanation* of existence, a
solution of the puzzle, an awakening from the night-
mare, so that all illusions may be dispelled and may
cease to distract the spirit.

A modern critic would at once perceive that what,
according to classic philosophy, happens by "chance",
gives us the key to all natural causation.   The tile
was loosened by the rain, or some other physical
agency; and the man passed by at that moment,
because minor incidents in that day's life had combined to bring him there.   That he could not have
prophesied that conjunction merely by proclaiming
his guiding impulses, or by defining the proper function of tiles, only proves that moral impulses and
functions are not primary causes, but tropes sustained
by the organization of animals or arts, which are a
part of nature; and that this animal or technical
organization remains in constant action and reaction
with the mechanical order of nature at large.   Any

"Truth" conceived to explain or annul the facts rather than to describe them.

prophecy founded on passion is therefore extremely loose and precarious: it can foresee at best that single strain in the future which will prolong the prophet's present impulses and powers. Accurate prophecy is possible only where the laws of matter have been studied, and the conjunction of various agencies in the future can be calculated. Amongst these agencies the organized powers and arts of man will be numbered; but circumstances must be reckoned with. The issue will always be partly determined by what the moralist calls "chance"; and the exact conjunction of particular "natures" and particular "chances" might be foretold by a science that had access to all the circumstances.

In regard to "eternal truths", a modern critic, if imperfectly critical, might be inclined merely to substitute natural laws or mathematical logic for the intuitive principles proclaimed by the prophets; but in so doing he would confuse, as the prophets do, the intrinsic eternity of all truth with the length of time *Natural laws proclaimed prophetically to be "eternal truths".* during which a particular fact, or a particular trope, may prevail in nature. An "eternal truth" would then mean an everlasting fact; but as the everlastingness of any fact can only be presumed, and as the future or the unknown past might well belie that presumption, "eternal truths" would become presumptive also, and mere articles of faith. Such, indeed, these logical pillars of the universe appear to be when we consider them critically: notions in origin, postulates in function, abstractions in character, and probably not truths at all.

The demands of sanity, though not of logic, were satisfied by this classical philosophy. The nature of things and "eternal truths" determined the future as well as the past, but only within limits. The outlines were fixed, rational, and predictable; but the

H

detail was due to "chance", and there was no knowing how it would befall. Therefore Aristotle and

But what
the future
will be is
predictable
only if we
admit mech-
anism or
Providence.

his pagan followers could deny the truth
of propositions about the future: human
predictions of chance events were superstitious, whilst the divine mind possessed
only general ideas and was sublimely
ignorant of all accidents, whether future or
past. On the other hand, no pervasive mechanical
laws were admitted by which many of these accidents, or all of them in theory, might be calculated
backwards and forwards, in contempt of moralistic
categories. Yet this possibility, well known to the
ancient atomists, was destined to prove fertile in
modern science, and to seem the key to nature; while
the intense personal religion of the monotheists
demanded a God who should be the sole creator and
ruler of the world, and the searcher of all hearts, to
their most secret depths. A God who did not foresee the consequences of his acts would be a blind
natural force; and one who exercised only an involun-
tary influence, and thought of nothing but his own
thinking, would be too evidently a cold figment of
logic. Monotheism thus introduced into the popular
mind, in an inevitably mythical form, the radical
notions of matter and of truth. Divine omnipotence
stood for matter, or the universal dynamic agency in
the world; and divine omniscience stood for the truth,
eternal and comprehensive.

In being personified, however, these ontological
principles were united incongruously, and the notion
of truth in particular came to be entangled in artificial
difficulties. The truth is not a power, only a description of the works of power, be they what they will.
The truth about the future does not therefore compel
the future to be what it will be, but on the contrary,
the character of that future, due to no matter what

causes, or perhaps quite causeless, compels the truth about it to be what that truth eternally is. This was often perceived by theologians in the controversies concerning freedom and necessity. Divine foreknowledge did not influence what it foresaw; but this consideration, though just, was futile, because the omnipotence of God, combined with his foreknowledge, did after all render him responsible for everything foreseen. If we drop the mythical element and consider truth and power in their respective essences, this complication disappears. Truth is absolutely passive, following all the contingent meanderings of existence; and whether these are spanned by large or by small tropes, or rebellious to all measure, is a question of fact for which existence itself must supply the answer. This answer will be the truth.

CHAPTER XII

LOVE AND HATRED OF TRUTH

THE love of truth is often mentioned, the hatred of truth hardly ever, yet the latter is the commoner.

Truth naturally hated rather than loved. People say they love the truth when they pursue it, and they pursue it when unknown: not therefore because of any felt affinity to it in their souls, but probably because they need information for practical purposes, or to solve some conventional riddle. Where known, on the contrary, truth is almost always dismissed or disguised, because the aspect of it is hateful. And this apart from any devilish perversity in the natural man, or accidental vices that may fear the light. On the contrary, the cause is rather the natural man's innocence and courage in thinking himself the measure of all things. Life imposes selfish interests and subjective views on every inhabitant of earth: and in hugging these interests and these views the man hugs what he initially assumes to be the truth and the right. So that aversion from the real truth, a sort of antecedent hatred of it as contrary to presumption, is interwoven into the very fabric of thought.

Sense and fancy preempt belief. Images and feelings do not arise without a certain vital enthusiasm in forming or affirming them. To enjoy them is in some sense to hypostasize them and set them up as models to which other images and feelings should conform. A child will protest and be inwardly wounded if a story once told him is told differently the second

time. His little soul has accepted that world, and
needs to build upon it undisturbed. Sensation, which
makes the foreground of what is called experience,
is thus raised by innocent faith to the level of truth.
And false these images and feelings would not be, if
they provoked no assertions about further objects.
They would compose the ingredients of a true biography, although perhaps, when the circumstances
are considered, the biography of a dupe.

Now love is a passion, and we might expect it
not to be aroused at all by intellectual objects, such
as truth, or theory purporting to be true: and yet the
bitterest feuds, in families and nations, often turn on
the love or hatred of particular beliefs, attacked or
defended for the most fantastic reasons. Both sides
may perhaps say that they are fighting for the truth;
but evidently it is not any circumstantial evidence
that supports the claims of the opposed ideas to be
veridical; nor is there often much intrinsic beauty in
those ideas. The theological notion of the Trinity
was little affected by that iota for which nevertheless
blood flowed in the streets of Byzantium; yet the
metaphysical dignity of the Virgin Mary was involved,
and nobody should be suffered to question the truth
of a devout image so fondly lodged in the mind.

In such a case the passion concerned is not the
love of truth, but a natural joy in thinking freely,
and the self-assertion of each mind against all others.
If meantime any attention is paid to the truth at all,
it is only indirectly, in that the ideal authority of
truth is recognized, whilst, by an absurd contradiction,
its verdict is dictated to it by violence. The truth
is needed, but not respected, not loved but raped;
and that barbarous outrage to the truth in the concrete
is still a sort of homage to truth as the coveted sanction
of fancy.

Modern philosophers seem hardly aware of the

extent to which they still reason on these principles. *Occam's Razor*, for instance, or economy as a criterion of truth, is the weapon of a monstrous self-mutilation with which British philosophy, if consistent, would soon have committed suicide. Only if all ideas were condemned to be blind and ugly, like a secret telegraphic code, would there be a human advantage in having the fewest and the baldest ideas possible: a gain, even then, only because thinking would be a loss, a waste of energy to be reduced to the practicable minimum. As to the truth of simple rather than elaborate ideas, what evidence does nature or history afford for such a presumption? Is nature sparing of atoms or seeds, of depths of organization and interrelation beyond the reach of human thought? Doubtless when applied to scholastic entities, conceived as dominant elements or powers (conceived, that is, as limiting the exuberance and waste in nature), Occam's Razor might serve to clear the ground for a richer crop of ideas. But for what ideas? I see no lilies of the field, I see only an expanse of coal-dust.

Parsimony in thinking shows indifference to truth.

In fact, most scholastic distinctions were made in the effort to clarify the mind, and bring language nearer to the precise relations of things. This philosophy was not experimental physics; it did not trace the movements of matter on their own plane; it studied rather the functions that things might have in the life of reason, as classic rhetoric and morals had defined that life. Such humanism was itself a monument to self-complacency in the home mind and aversion from arctic and torrid truth; but at least in its own dimension it was diligent. So are modern mathematics and physics, to a degree that renders them more inventive and unintelligible than any philosophy; but though many of their terms, or all, may be figments of human method, they play respect-

fully round the profound complexity of things; and
there is more modesty and love of truth in the better
men of science than in the old scholastics, in that
they admit that their conventions are largely arbitrary
and symbolic.

A false truth is often attributed to human ideas,
even when they are not taken for physical objects or
powers. Æsthetic, moral or political sentiments, for instance, because they arouse a
certain enthusiasm, are proclaimed as truths;
individuals and parties entrench themselves
within those maxims with all the ferocity of
hatred and fear: hatred and fear of the
besieging reality, that would prove that no such feelings can express any objective truth, but only the
life of some biological or political organism. That
every organism must have its own form of life and
must love and defend it, goes without saying: but
why poison the inevitable conflict of possible forms
by insulting your rivals, and saying they have no
right to attempt to live? Courage, that in a rational
being would be courteous, then borrows the blindness
and useless cruelty of instinct; and the legitimate
will to live usurps the authority of destiny, which
determines what forms of life, at any time and place,
may actually prosper. Truly great men, nobly dominant wills, appeal, indeed, to that authority of destiny
which they feel working within them: and common
moralizing does the same thing when, without anger
or false threats, it points to the vanity of some ambitions
and the miserable consequences of some vices.

Plato reports the humorous saying of Socrates that
dogs are philosophical because they bark at strangers,
thereby showing how much they prize knowledge.
Intentionally or unintentionally there is a play here
upon the word knowledge. This name is given at
once, and sophistically, both to familiarity and to

Pre-rational morality asserts its intuitions in defiance of moral truth.

understanding; so that fondness for what we happen to know and hostility towards what we happen not to know are identified with the love of truth. Yet in fact they are the exact opposite. What we and the dogs love is our safety, our home-thoughts, our illusions and our undisputed confidence in habit. Undoubtedly, in controversial moments, we defend our ideas under the name of great and evident truths, as we defend our worldly possessions under the name of natural rights. In this we manifest our animal nature, like faithful dogs, and are biologically admirable and morally blameless. There is indeed something candid and honest in trusting appearance and in being loyal to convention; but to be dogged about these things with a clear conscience is hardly possible to an intelligent man. A dull child may tell the truth without understanding it, not in the least for the love of truth, but simply for lack of alternatives. Had he a less sluggish imagination he might have invented some aimless lie. Stupidity is positivistic, and sometimes, as in science, literal and uninterpreted reports are useful; they are trustworthy as far as they go, and allow us to do our own thinking. For the thinking spirit, however, literalness is simple slavery to appearance or to convention on the level of sense; a slavery that an intellectual coward may sometimes love. It saves him from discovering a truth secretly felt to be inhuman.

Sensuous appearance and spontaneous language are nevertheless far from hostile to the truth: they are first steps in the pursuit of it. Nature takes good care to discredit our young idolatries, and drives us from one image to another, from each thought to some alternative thought. Not, or not often, by the force of logic, which indeed would rather tighten its coils about us, and enclose us in an impenetrable

Attachment to familiar ideas shows love not of truth but of comfort.

Fear of being deceived is again not a love of truth but of safety.

cocoon of its own weaving. Conviction always abounds in its own sense, as in theology: but what breaks at last through such a charmed circle is wild nature, within and without. A thousand contrary facts, a thousand rebel emotions, drive us from our nest. We find that *there can be no peace in delusion*: and perhaps in this negative and moral guise the idea of truth first insinuates itself into the mind. No spiritual understanding, no generous interest in the truth on its own level and for its own sake: only discomfort in uncertainty, uneasiness about things hidden, and a prudent concern for the future. In positing the future and the hidden and also the past, we have already posited truth, but blindly, without distinguishing intellectually truth, which we might discover and possess, from facts extinct or unborn or incommunicable. We do not in the least care to discover or possess the truth; but we wish to be armed to face the obdurate facts; and our pride recoils from the confusion of finding ourselves mistaken. Better, then, examine everything suspiciously and form no idea, as we should buy no clothes, not likely to wear well. Hence a certain shrewdness and prudence in conceiving matters closely affecting us, each man in his own trade, each woman in her own circle; but this specialized sagacity is remote from the love of truth not only in motive but in scope. The foundation is laid in egotism, in partiality, in injustice; enormous tracts of relevant reality are wilfully ignored; and the result is some slander or some party tenet or some superstition, defended pugnaciously rather because it is preciously false than because it is presumably true. The more these self-indulgent minds fear and hate the truth, the more insistently they give the name of truth to the mask that hides it.

That fiction and convention should usurp in this manner the authority of truth—an authority which, however ideal it may be, is logically absolute—naturally arouses the ire of the critical; and it is not without reason that individual investigators, re-formers, and heretics feel that they are champions of the truth. They are, in fact, rebels against imposture. Yet they ordin-arily have many stronger and nearer motives for their zeal than love of truth for its own sake: love of ideas, novelties, adventure, controversy, and power. Take the case where bias and ulterior motives seem most radically absent: the case of the scientific empiricist, a compass in one hand and a balance in the other. He may say he is pursuing pure truth. Yet an exact record of his experiments would hardly disclose any-thing more enlightening than would the sights and gossip of the street. They would be glimpses and gossip about matter, not about human affairs: and this is far from implying that the glimpses or gossip would be truer. On the contrary, it is precisely about the social world that a man's surface impressions are apt to be adequate: the object is like the medium. And indeed the scientific man is not likely to be satisfied with the bare record of his experiments, which would report the strict truth of his investiga-tion. Instead, every experiment will suggest to him some new theory, or will seem to illustrate and confirm some old theory familiar to his mind. So fortified, he may be doubly ready to denounce the errors of his more conventional neighbours, whom he probably dislikes on other grounds, and wishes to supersede in public estimation. Nor is this always the merely inevitable admixture of different passions in a human being. The pure theory advanced is not likely in the end to be truer than the views it replaces. It is often truer in some particular; but when its tendency and oversights are considered, it very seldom increases the harmony between man and nature. Perhaps if

Criticism is dogma on a different level.

critical and empirical motives governed science absolutely, science would disappear. Autobiography would
replace it, with a perfect democracy of theories, as
so many idle ideas, going with different moods; and
when memory and solipsism had been criticized in
their turn, the so-called zeal for truth would end by
denying the notion of truth altogether.

That would be the second childhood of the mind.
Instead of innocent joy in appearance and in language,
as if nothing could be false, there would be But all
a collapse into idiocy, as if nothing could be dogmas
true. Vigorous critics and innovators are posit, and
far from such apathy. They strip off one honour, the
mask of truth only to substitute another, truth.
as the truer image: and they very likely join the elder
dogmatists in maintaining that in the mask they propose the likeness to the original is perfect. Not all
an honest man's zeal, be he a traditionalist or a reformer,
is arrested at the specific doctrines which he identifies
with the truth: the better part pierces that symbol and
rests in the truth itself, pure and absolute, which
wears that mask for him for the moment. So that
all is not hypocrisy in this partisan or fantastic zeal.
Within the fanatical defence of vested illusions there
may be a sacrificial respect for things beyond us,
whatever those secret realities may be; and the martyr
that on earth is ready to die for some false opinion
may be judged in heaven to have died for the truth.
The very absurdity of a tenet, or its groundlessness,
at least proves that imagination is at work, and groping
for an issue from animal darkness. At least the category of truth has been set up. Appearances, innocent
and perfectly real in themselves, have begun to be
questioned and discounted as deceptive; and this not
merely against the blank background of a posited
substance, known only as a force, but in contrast to
a possible and more adequate description of that

substance and of the manner in which it produces appearances. Intelligence has begun the pursuit of truth.

Does this pursuit ever really deserve the name of love? No doubt there must be a total and exact collocation of facts, and the universe must have a form which we call the truth of it; but why should anyone *love* that collocation, in its perhaps infinite and certainly inhuman minuteness and extent? Why should anyone desire to know what that tiresome truth may be, except for human purposes in the region and on the scale of our gross experience? We may love our pleasures, our perceptions, our dogmas; we may love safety and dominion in action, and victory in argument; but if the truth is none of these things, why should we love it?

Why should respect for truth turn into love ?

There is no *reason* why we should love the truth. There is no *reason* why we should love anything. There are only causes that, according to the routine of nature, bring about the love of various things on various occasions. As a matter of fact, nature breeds life, and life is everywhere aflame with love, and with its opposite; and there is also no reason why this spiritual passion—spiritual because it engages and colours the spirit—should stop short at bodily concerns or social affairs, and should not extend to all the relations radiating from bodily life into the realms of truth and of essence. This radiation, as I call it, is in itself passive and merely formal, yet physical organization must take account of it if life is to prosper; and this tension of life towards the eventual, the distant, the past and the future is what becomes conscious and bursts into actuality in spirit. Spirit is a child of truth. Matter in any one of its moments and in any one of its atoms offers no foothold for

The forward strain or cosmic Eros in all existence becomes conscious in spirit.

consciousness: but let certain tropes and cycles be established in the movement of matter, let certain kinds of matter cohere and pulse together in an organism, and behold, consciousness has arisen. Now tropes, cycles, organisms, and pulsations, with all the laws of nature, are units proper to the realm of truth; units that bridge the flux of existence and are suspended over it, as truth and spirit also are suspended. So that in conceiving and loving the truth spirit is not indulging in any caprice; it is surveying with pleasure the soil and the broad reaches of its native country.

Nor is love too warm a term for the sense of this radical affinity. There is cosmic justification for such a passion. Love is, biologically, an emotion proper to generation: and generation, in the cosmos at large, is the same thing as genesis or flux. Love, ever since Hesiod and Empedocles, has therefore been the poetic name for the instability and fecundity of transitive existence everywhere; life passing, and passing joyfully, from each phase to the next, and from one individual to another. Yet this joyful procreation of things is also tragic, because as Lucretius says, nothing is born save by the death of something else. In loving, in breeding, and in bringing up the young we make an unconscious sacrifice of ourselves to posterity. Such is the dominance of love in the realm of matter, where progression is, as it were, horizontal, and the thing generated continues and repeats the nature of its parents. But where the transmitted form is organic, and spirit inhabits it, life and love have also a vertical direction and a synthetic power, such that in precipitating the future, the present evokes some image of the past, and some notion of the outlying realities by which the present and the future are being controlled. In other words, life, in propagating itself, has also generated knowledge, and has become aware of the truth.

This by-product or hypostasis of organic life is also tragic, like physical reproduction, and accepts death; but instead of surrendering one life for another of the same kind and on the same level, we now surmount or disregard physical life altogether, in order to define its form and consider its achievements. This consideration or definition of nature is itself a work of nature, occurring in time and requiring material organs. It therefore partakes of the joy proper to all vital functions in their perfection. The beauty of truth is loved as naturally as the beauty of women, and our ideas are cherished like our children. Enthusiasm and inspiration (which are other names of love addressed to the truth) have no less warmth and breed no less heroism than the love of home or of country.

And transcends the flux ideally by conceiving it.

Thus spirit is born and chooses its aims in sympathy with the movement of organic life, and is simply that movement become emotion and idea. For this radical reason spirit cannot be an independent power coming from nowhere to direct or accelerate animal action. We do not look about us because we love the truth, but we love the truth because we look about us. Were it merely a question of keeping alive or of controlling matter, business would actually be expedited if besides Occam's razor we used, so to speak, Occam's glasses, and reduced our visions of things to pointer-readings, releasing appropriate reactions on our part without further rhetoric. Ignorance, when not materially dangerous, simplifies the fighting mind and is an economic advantage. It renders courage absolute and disturbs no comfortable or harmless illusions. Nature, however, being spontaneous and free, with no end of time before her, despises such thrift and is initially lavish and all-consenting. Her indefinite passive fertility is com-

This movement automatically assigns intrinsic value to truth.

mitted to no antecedent prejudices or desires. She
adopts her laws and types unwittingly, as they avail
to establish themselves; and they leave untouched her
original potentialities. They may become, indeed,
positive occasions for playful complications far outrunning those special terms and eluding their measure.
Such a complication life seems to us to be in respect
to mechanism, and consciousness in respect to life.
In these cases the new fruit, while having an underiv-
able character proper to itself, will draw all its existential sap from the tree on which it is grafted. Life
requires food, warmth and air, yet is none of those
things but an organization accruing to them; and
spirit feeds on the life of the psyche, while establish-
ing tangential and transcendent interests of its own.
When feeling (a form of spirit evoked by organic
processes in the body) becomes perception and begins
to describe the objects that arouse feeling, spirit is
already launched upon the pursuit of truth, an ideal
reality altogether transcending the level of the psyche
and of her world. When, moreover, the eye and the
intellect have adequately surveyed the scene, or
gathered the event observed into a dramatic unity,
the organ of spirit is satisfied. It is satisfied in the
very act by which a truth is discerned; so that by
nature this discernment is a joy to the spirit, and
the truth automatically conceived becomes an object
of love for its own sake.

The vital and fundamentally physical quality of
this love of truth appears clearly when it is thwarted.
We see daily in young children and in   To stop
impatient reformers how nothing is more   short of
the truth
hateful to a passionate being than obstruc-   is a vital
tion, nothing more precious than liberty.   frustration.
The psyche will have her way in the first place, let
the result be what it will.   Indeed, the primitive horror
of being stifled, of being held down and prevented

from moving, is doubtless what lends its magic to the word liberty: any idea of what we might do with our liberty when we got it would have no such power. To be checked in our natural actions before we initiate them produces melancholy: to be checked in the middle of them produces rage. This intolerableness of suppression extends to the movement of our thoughts. It was in the act of spinning fine long threads of relationship that nature first evoked spirit: that web must not be torn, and nature demands that spirit should think the truth. We cannot endure to be cheated, to be deluded, even to suspect that we are deceiving ourselves. We may be incurious about remote truths, if our intellect is lazy; but at least we would not stultify what intellect we have by believing things positively false. Therefore when authority or public opinion would hold us down to some manifest error, however harmless and metaphysical, our impetuous souls resent the outrage. It is not the calm truth that calls for witnesses: martyrs usually die for some new error. It is the martyrs that cannot endure in themselves the arrest of the heart upon thoughts that the heart despises. No matter how tragic or arid the truth may be, the spirit follows and loves it, as the eye follows the light.

Automatic as the love of truth is, and internal as is the joy of discovering and holding the truth, this love has nothing narcissistic about it. It is as far as possible from being joy in the lustre or harmony of one's ideas. It is a clean, healthy, sacrificial love. In the form of childish curiosity it is turned from the beginning towards alien things, engaging the impulse to explore, to dissect, and to dare. The element of courage, united with submission and humility, belongs to the love of truth even in its ultimate reaches. Truth, in spite of what Platonists

Yet the standard of truth remains external and the love of truth is a form of worship.

and poets may say, is not at all the same as beauty. Truth does not arrange or idealize its subject-facts. It can eliminate nothing. It can transfigure nothing, except by merely lifting it bodily from the plane of existence and exhibiting it, not as a present lure or as a disaster for some native ambition, but as a comedy or tragedy seen as a whole and liberating the spirit that understands it. In other words, truth is a moral, not an æsthetic good. The possession of it is not free intuition, but knowledge necessary to a man's moral integrity and intellectual peace.

That conventional truths, as exhibited to the senses, or in historical narrative or scientific exposition, may often be impressive æsthetically goes without saying: but it is not this æsthetic quality that makes their truth or satisfies the intellect. If truth at first entertains, as falsehood does also, it very soon sobers and rebukes. It is tragic even in comedy, since it looks to the end of every career and every achievement. The very movement of instinctive exploration that discloses truth, thereby discloses also the relativity, limits, and fugitiveness of this exploration. It shows life under the form of eternity, which is the form of death. Life thereby becomes an offering, a prayer, a sacrifice offered up to the eternal; and though there may be incense in that sacrifice, there is also blood.

Such affinity as there is between truth and beauty has various sources. When the word truth is coloured idealistically, to mean the types or potential perfections of things, as when we speak of a true friend, evidently if this latent "truth" could only be brought out and raised to actual fact, it would also realize the beautiful. Love and charity are quick to perceive the latent perfections of the imperfect; and if we call this (perhaps imaginary) potentiality the truth, we indeed divine the principle of beauty also; of that beauty which the

The true is akin to the beautiful when it means "true to type".

I

organic impulses of nature would bring to light if they had their way and did not interfere with one another.

Even this partial chaos and mutual destruction, when we see it to be the truth, for the very reason that we are interested in the beauties des- troyed, has a cathartic effect. It is sublime; and if we call the sublime a part of the beautiful, the truth, even when distressing and ugly, will be horribly beautiful to us. Both naturalism and romanticism work this vein of merciless poetry. Religion often does the same thing indirectly, and aided by myths: the heart is taught to transmute its affections, so as to make them consonant with the will of God, that is, with the truth. But here we may see the danger of forced assimilations of the true to the good or to the beautiful. False views are often called true, in order to make the truth more consoling; and on the other hand moral and æsthetic values are often distorted by being torn from their roots in an animal soil and stretched on a rack of cosmic dimensions. The starry spaces bring us face to face with depths of reality hidden by the light of day: we find that spectacle beautiful, and sublime in its inhumanity; and the better part of our humanity then seems to be our capacity to rise above ourselves. But it is in fact one part of us that here eludes or rebukes another part. Nature is necessarily full of beauties, since our faculties of perception and sympathy would not subsist if they were not adapted to the facts of nature; and the truth is necessarily satisfying, for the same reason. Yet nature is also full of ugly, cruel and horrible things, and the truth in many ways is desolating: because our nature, though sufficiently harmonious with the universe to exist within it, is nevertheless finite and specific, with essential interests which nature

Also when the beautiful turns to the sublime or over- whelming.

and truth at large cannot but disregard. The truth, then, is often, in many ways, interesting, beautiful and sublime: but it is not identical with beauty either in quality or extension or status.

Undoubtedly, in their different ways, truth and beauty are both liberating; and when mystics identify them it may be because they are exalted by both above the travail of existence. In the case of beauty this deliverance is spontaneous and innocent: the spirit takes wing at birth, and flutters from flower to flower, without suspecting that any other fate awaits it. But the deliverance that comes through the truth comes through sorrow: it is redemption by the cross. The more inhuman the truth turns out to be, the more dismal or cruel, so much greater is the self-conquest involved in facing it, in casting away false hopes, and entrenching ourselves impregnably in our insignificance. The very act of recognizing our insignificance, if sincere and not a mask for new claims, removes the sting of that insignificance. There is even something sadistic in the pleasure with which certain religious minds gloat on their own misery, as if they could never trample enough on their bleeding hearts or dance enough on their graves. But there is no occasion to exaggerate. To be finite is not a sin, to be ignorant is not a disgrace: the pleasures of illusion and those of disillusion are equally human. Pure insight into truth surmounts human bias in both directions impartially, without in the least hating or condemning the life that involves such bias; for to hate or condemn finitude is as finite as to cling to any particular form of finitude with an absolute fury. Intuition is liberating on every level, in each case defining the proper and adequate object of the faculty concerned. In sensation, intuition liberates some essence from the obscurity and tangle of fact; from passion it liberates

Also in freeing the spirit from private entanglements.

eloquence, poetry and beauty; from the known world it liberates truth. The operation of each faculty, so perfected, turns into clear joy. To take the full measure of anything, especially of anything living, establishes (quite apart from practical advantages) a spiritual dominion over that thing. You have seen it, you have seen through it, you have seen round it. It no longer can hold you to any weak or unmerited regard. It no longer can torture you with a useless hatred. Moreover, in partly lifting your ignorance, the truth has liberated you from avidity for knowledge. Fortune can never unveil to you more than a part of the truth: such part as is important for you and as you can digest. This part, seen under the form of eternity, can then cease to be external to you; it can become a term and familiar rhythm in your own life. And this part of your life, being absorbed in pure intuition, will no longer seem consciously yours, nor concerned with your personal fortunes. It will be a light revealing the truth to you, and will be lost in the eternity of that which it knows.

Nevertheless, in the dead season of the mind, when every generous faculty is paralysed, it may become incredible that an immaterial reality, or material unreality, like the truth should ever be prized or even conceived. This doubt or denial is incidental to intellectual decay; but that fact does not count from the point of view of the decadence. We must therefore examine the position from within, in its subjective origin and logic.

CHAPTER XIII

DENIALS OF TRUTH

PILATE'S question, *What is truth?* might be asked with varying intentions. It might be a sincere enquiry, assuming that the word truth stood for something assignable, and asking what that thing exactly was. A sincere answer might then be forthcoming, such for instance as is contained in this book. Very likely, however, the original demand would not have concerned so abstract a subject as the ontological nature of truth, considered as a logical category. The question would rather have touched what might be true in the concrete, in some such matter as religion or scientific theory; and then an adequate answer would be wellnigh endless, involving all conventional human knowledge.

The nature of truth in the abstract and in the concrete is largely ascertainable.

Pilate, however, and those who have repeated his question were probably not desirous of learning anything. Their question was merely an exclamation of impatience, uttered in mockery or bravado, or perhaps in despair. If the sentiment were despair, it might be as honest as the innocent desire to know: in both cases we should be assuming the definite reality of the truth, in the one case by looking for it hopefully, and in the other case by thinking of it so grandly and placing it at so great a remove that the hope of ever possessing it would seem to us chimerical. Yet this honest kind of despair could only be momentary, and occasioned

Despair about it a passing mood.

by some inordinate ambition to know all truth or to know the most comprehensive truths infallibly: something not consonant with the nature and station of man. Disappointment there, though sharp, would soon yield to contentment with such knowledge as is natural to us, and humanly interesting. Truth near home, in many a detail, is continually revealed to us; we cannot open a door or receive the answer to a letter without finding verified sundry assumptions made currently by instinct, and being assured that, in some sense, they were true. Amongst these familiar truths any educated man will place the elements of geography, biology, and history: and these, if his mind is open and unprejudiced, will suffice to show him the place of man in nature, the character of his organs of sense, and the images formed by these organs, together with the general history of human opinion. In view of these facts he would become aware that all human *knowledge* of truth, by virtue of its seat and function, must be relative and subjectively coloured. It expresses the sensations and expectations of a specific animal. It is therefore vastly different both in extent and in texture from the literal and complete truth about the universe.

This relativism no doubt shocks and humbles the spontaneously poetic mind. Spirit is initially addressed to omniscience, as it is to perfect freedom and happiness, and even to absolute power. These sweeping ambitions are involved in the synthetic character of spirit, in its moral warmth and in its cognitive transcendence, in idea, over remote times and places; also in its inevitable isolation or egotism: and the same ambitions are encouraged by the real æsthetic and dialectical fertility of mind, when once an organism has flowered into consciousness, and begun to dream. To find itself harnessed to facts that it cannot control, to find

Primitive dogmatism must be renounced.

itself helpless and mistaken, is therefore a hard lesson
for the spirit.   But this chastening is not fatal; on the
contrary, it is positively enlightening and steadying.
Not only does appropriate knowledge, in picturesque
and infinite vistas, remain open, but spirit can now
bring order into its own house, and consecrate itself
to its essential vocation without being distracted by
vain hopes.

Far, however, from denying or doubting the being
of truth, such relativism as to knowledge doubly asserts
it.   On the one hand, it presupposes much *Criticism of*
true information about nature and human *knowledge*
life; because criticism, even if we call it *doubly reaffirms*
scepticism, is founded on knowledge.   On *the reality*
the other hand, the reality of an unknown *of truth.*
truth beyond the human sphere is thereby asserted
emphatically and even pathetically: we should not
need to beweep our ignorance if there were nothing to
know.   The post-religious agnosticism widespread in
the nineteenth century was suffering from the vacuum
left by a lost faith in revelation: in pottering about
amongst appearances, and talking about science and
progress, it felt secretly empty and bereaved.   The
truth, which had seemed to shine so warm and near
upon a former age, had receded to an infinite distance
and been eclipsed for ever.   The agnostics often felt
some tenderness for their lost illusions: and what they
smiled at bitterly, and regarded as inexcusable, was
rather the impudence of lay philosophers who ventured
to proclaim the absolute truth of their toy systems.
That was a double insult to the wise and the sorrowful:
it ignored the depths of nature about us; it ignored
also the depths of imagination and religion within us,
by which the old faith had been inspired.   As belief
in the reality of material objects is never more acute
than in the dark, when we are groping cautiously and
intently amongst them, so the reality of overarching

truth was never more painfully acknowledged than by these agnostics, conscious of not being able to define its form.

Luckily, honest agonies are brief. We become callous to ignorance, as we do to poverty, danger, or solitude: and presently a new healthy equilibrium is established in the mind. Custom and necessity carry us bodily along in conventional speech and action; we live with our images and metaphors without prying too closely into their credentials, as we live with our friends. And if in speculative moments misgivings overtake us, either we deliberately cover our heads with the hood of resignation, or perhaps we are visited by some sudden revelation and conspire with ourselves to trust it. In either case, whether by abstinence or divination, we join mankind in positing a comprehensive and inviolate truth hanging above us, and making our falsehoods false and our truths true.

In Pilate's question, however, we may detect a subtler and more insidious suggestion. He feels he *The real* has hold of nothing, and he mocks reality. *challenge to* Mockery is a means of restoring our self-*truth lies in* *blind* respect by universalizing our own hollow-*impulse.* ness. As if he said: *Did I ever trouble about truth? No. Then why are these fools talking about it? The truth is that there is no truth.*

Self-contradiction could not be franker. Evidently to deny the truth is to make an assertion, and thereby *That which* to allege that there is a truth. Yet a formal *is denied* refutation of this sort remains rather puerile. *and may* *be absent* It would ignore the depth of irritation and *is not* animal courage in that self-contradiction, the *truth but* *knowledge* scorn of words, the reversion to primitive *of truth.* slumber. Even on the rational level, the verbal contradiction may be easily removed by a *distinguo* which is itself necessary and important. In saying, "The truth is that there is no truth", we use the word truth in two different senses. In the first clause "truth" means the truth; in the second clause it means *knowledge* of the truth. Now the truth might well be that there were no true human opinions or criteria of certainty: and although a Cretan may not properly say that all Cretans are always liars, a laughing god might say so with perfect consistency. In fact the truth has a superhuman status: so that an absence of true opinions or criteria would not in the least abolish it. Moreover, spirit, which also is human only by accident and may forget its physical seat, can readily conceive an experience that should be inwardly irrelevant to truth altogether, so that within that experience there should be no problems, no alleged true opinions, and no category of truth or of error. It would suffice that such an experience should remain æsthetic and should never posit any removed object, even any removed part of itself. Music, for instance, is in this case: and if certain philosophies, like fine arts, aspire to the condition of music, they actually aspire not indeed to deny but to forget the truth. Of course the most irresponsible dance of feelings and images would be shadowed in all its convolutions by the truth about it, as any existence is inevitably shadowed; but it need not see its own shadow; it need never stop to consider the truth about itself. If the word truth fell somehow from outside into those buzzing ears, the retort might come from within with perfect sincerity: *There is no truth.*

Such, I think, would be the only radical and wholly honest denial of truth: an avowal that, in one's own mind, the notion of truth was absent and needless. Great multitudes of animals would doubtless say so, if they could speak. But in human philosophy the denial of truth is something late and artificial, a contorted, confused, and villainous effort to squirm away from

Background of opportunism in belief.

one's intellectual conscience. In a compact society, where all the world is of one opinion, the worldling will be cocksure of the truth; but when society is loose and decadent, why should he commit himself to any one of a thousand conflicting, exacting, and narrowing systems? To choose rationally he would need to dig down to first principles: but to what first principles? He is probably decayed himself at the core, and can find no first principles there. His obvious course is then to choose at each turn whatever views may be convenient, and to proclaim that there is no truth.

Civilizations are often partly rotten before they are ripe; so that chronologically there may be no great interval between the sophists who deny the being of truth and the philosophers who endeavour to piece the truth together or to defend it, as it may have inspired an earlier age. Thus in Greece the chief Sophists were hardly later than the chief naturalists and law-givers, and earlier than Socrates, Plato, and Aristotle.

In respect to truth the two famous sayings reported of Protagoras suffice to set the essential problem.
The maxims of Protagoras. "Man," he said, "is the measure of all things, of that which is, that it is, and that which is not, that it is not." And he also said, "True is what appears to each man at each moment." I am not concerned with the historical question, vain and insoluble in itself, as to what may have been the exact connotation of these phrases in their author's mind. I take them as public property, to be turned to the best uses of which they are still capable. The first maxim will serve admirably for the first principle of humanism. Humanism begins in the moral sphere, with the perception that every man's nature is, for him, the arbiter of values. So far, this view merely universalizes the Gospel text that the Sabbath was made for man and not man for the Sabbath. From such moral enlightenment, however, we may easily slip into

equivocations that will land us in moral chaos. In saying that a man's *nature* is, for him, the arbiter of values, we may understand that nothing is good or bad but *thinking* makes it so. We shall then have confused what a man is with what he thinks he is, and identified his interests with his wishes. Under cover of freedom to be ourselves we shall be denying that we have any true nature; and under cover of asserting our native rights we shall be denying that we have any ultimate interests. Humanism, so understood, will have disintegrated humanity, declared all passions equally good and proclaimed moral anarchy.

These equivocations may extend beyond the sphere of morals and may end in identifying all reality with consciousness. The first maxim of Prota- Moral goras, that *man* is the criterion, will have anarchy become equivalent to his second maxim, extended that the criterion is the present *moment*. intellect. Yet even in regard to the present moment there is a serious ambiguity. The word which I have translated by "appears," δοκεῖ, might rather mean "seems true", or "is thought to be true". If we took this second meaning seriously, far from denying the being of truth we should be regarding truth as omnipresent, and revealed by every thought or perception. In other words, we should be asserting that consciousness is never a passive feeling but always cognitive, capable of entertaining no appearance without regarding it as a description, and thinking it true. This may well be the case in action, when consciousness is on the wing and carried by animal faith to intend what is not given: but to make this self-transcendence universal would be the extreme of intellectualism, something impossible to attribute to Protagoras or to his modern emulators. Moreover, if all consciousness were cognitive, it could hardly be regarded as always veridical; and this claim to infallibility is only a playful or sarcastic way of saying that no opinion is true in a significant sense, because no moment of consciousness can have a removed object but must necessarily regard only the image or idea then present to the mind. For this reason I have rendered the term used by Protagoras by "appears" rather than by "seems true" or "is thought to be true"; because the ultimate position can hardly be other than this: that when that which appears is thought true the appearance becomes an illusion; and that this appearance is true only in the sense that it verily appears: in which sense all appearances are true equally.

The Greek Sophists were great men of the world addressing little men of the world: they could not be expected to push scepticism into the sphere of common sense; its use was merely to discredit speculation and authority. The Greeks in general were given to speech-making before the crowd. They might cast ridicule on all reported knowledge, and raise a laugh: they could hardly expect to carry their audience with them, if they denied the existence of that audience, or the intimate shrewd ratiocinations of each man in the crowd, hugging his own thoughts and his own interests. Therefore the unchallenged and unexpressed presuppositions of all criticism in this school must be the existence of conventional human society and the intelligent egoism of each of its members. All else in heaven and earth might be challenged with applause, if reduced to these comfortable and convincing terms.

This denial of truth assumes the truth of psychologism.

Was the being of truth, then, denied by the Sophists, or could they deny it? Yes, if we think only of the truth as proclaimed by particular opinions. All things *said* to be true might be false. Whatsoever depended on argument might be challenged by an opposed cleverer argument; whatsoever depended on usage,

Personal pride hid this from the ancients.

faith, or preference might be reversed by a contrary pose; so that every man remained free to think and do what he liked, and to deny all authority.   This, though with a different moral tone and intention, was also the position of the Sceptics.   They despised opinion, and collected contradictory arguments in order to liberate the mind from every pledge and the heart from every earthly bond.   These indomitable doubters stood firm as rocks in their philosophy; and even the Sophists were sure of their wisdom and knowingness in playing their chosen parts in the world.   For both schools, then, there was an *unspoken truth*: namely, that life was a treacherous predicament in which they found themselves without a reason, and that they were determined, whether nobly or nimbly, to make the best of it.   Their moral philosophy left the cosmos problematical, while taking for granted abundant knowledge of human affairs and human character.   If that age had had a turn for introspection and autobiography, it might have erected a doctrine of the march of experience. Trust in memory, in expectation, in the mutual communication of many minds might have issued in a system like modern psychologism: the view that all we see, say, and think is false, but that the only truth is that we see, say and think it.   If nothing be real except experience, nothing can be true except biography.   Society must then be conceived as carried on in a literary medium, with no regard to the natural basis of society.   If the ancients never hit upon such a system of biographical metaphysics, the reason doubtless was that they were too intelligent.   In filling out their fragmentary natural knowledge with myths, they had originally invented other and more beautiful natural beings to help carry on the world: but when the conflict of theories had made the natural world seem problematical, they preferred to abstain from voluntary follies, and not to credit anything so fantastic

as that one sight or sound or pleasure or pain might
generate another in a vacuum. It mattered little how
events might be generated; the point was bravely to
enjoy and endure and mock them as they came. Such
spiritual courage, however, is physically barren.
Heroic scepticism soon withered, and officious sophistry
soon found nobody to listen to it. A new image of
truth was rising in the east, evoked by inspiration,
frankly miraculous, and destined to be sustained and
rekindled for ages only by faith.

The dominance of this imposing speculative doctrine, long identified with the truth, has caused the
Character denial of truth in modern times to assume
of modern a special character. It has seemed to go
scepticism. with enlightenment, with science, with the
pursuit of truth. How, indeed, should anyone pursue
the truth, if he were sure he possessed it? Trust in
inspiration is something retrograde: it reinstates the
primitive dogmatism of the senses, but reinstates it
on the imaginative plane, where the object is some
speculative idea or vision of the invisible, in regard to
which a clear faith is harder to maintain. Protestants
had freely criticized the doctrines of the Church, but
only by appealing to the infallible text of the Bible, or
to some new inspired image of the truth formed in
their private meditations; and each had claimed for his
shade of doctrine the authority of absolute truth. In
view of so many wrangling "truths", the wiser and
more humorous heads could not but distrust all con-
clusions. Free thought became romantic. Ever to
decide what you thought would be to stop thinking,
and the eternal search for the truth demanded that
you should never find it. But for a humanist or an
empiricist a truth never to be found differs little from
a nonentity. How then avoid the conviction that
fruitful science and adventurous philosophy imply a
denial that there is any such thing as truth?

This conviction, suggested by that chaos of inspired opinions which was the weak side of Protestantism, was fortified by what gave Protestantism its Refuge in strength—namely, subjective depth and sin- romantic cerity.   When sensuous dogmatism breaks subjectivity. down and we discover an optical illusion, *ipso facto* we discover a scientific truth; and we clarify the contrast, inherent in all investigation, between superficial appearance and material reality.   When on the contrary some illusion of the intellect is detected, or we lose faith in a revealed "truth", no other comparable conception is at hand to take the place of the discredited view. Revelation and "truth" go by the board together, and we are driven back upon immediate experience and the inner fountain of ideas.   These we must continue to accept, unless we should stop living; but we accept them now only as phenomena of life in ourselves, only as a kind of intellectual music which we cannot help making, because such is the fertility of our genius or the marvellous influence upon us of we know not what cosmic climate.

Some lurid romantic cloud land, in that case, truly envelops and contains us; and though the truth might then seem chaotic to us, because not amenable to our moral or grammatical categories, it would be nevertheless precisely the truth it was, and would display all our random visions and emotions precisely in their true places and true relativity.   We should then be talking nonsense when we said we denied the being of truth, this truth being avowedly, in respect to us, that we were in a plastic and ill-determined phase of intelligence, and honourably unwilling to pin our faith on any hasty dogma.

Thus as among the ancients, so among the moderns, the denial of truth is due to palpable confusions between truth and knowledge of truth, between essence and existence, between the ideal and the actual.   It might

seem that matters might easily be set right by recalling a few definitions. Yet these verbal equivocations
are not merely perverse: they are incidental
to slow voluminous shifts in morals and
culture. The truth posited by animal faith,
in action or in curiosity, is posited as unknown, as something to be investigated
and discovered; and truth in this transcendent sense
can never be denied by an active mind. But when
animal faith has already expressed itself in coventional
ideas, its own further action finds those ideas obstruc-
tive. Truth has now been rashly posited as known.
An idea, an idol, has taken the place of the god originally and intrinsically invoked by the mind, and posited
as unknown. But this is a scandal: how should the
thoughts of the wisest human head coincide with the
intrinsic essence of any object or event, not to speak
of the universe in its totality? The "truth" that the
critic or heretic then denies was itself a blasphemy,
and in denying it he is secretly animated by the love
of truth. What he denies is only the existence of any
view in which truth is contained once for all and
without qualification. Even if we admit prophecy and
supernatural inspiration, the most rapt of prophets can
only signalize, adumbrate, and clothe metaphorically
the truth revealed through his lips, and not fathomed
by his own rational mind: the most explicit of creeds
is called a symbol of the faith. The relation which
any such symbol may bear to the truth is evidently a
historical accident; and the more clearly we perceive
the inevitable, all-comprehensive, eternal being of
truth, the more improbable or even impossible must
seem the notion that any human conception should
ever do it justice.

To deny
the truth
reported
is to posit
the truth
unreported.

CHAPTER XIV

BEYOND TRUTH

THE temptation to deny the reality of truth does not often attack the mind. It is a suicidal tempta- tion that comes only in moments of surfeit or despair. Commoner and less easily mastered is the temptation to adorn the truth. Indeed, this is not so much a temptation as an original sin; because the truth never appears to us naked, but clothed and masked in sensa- tions and in language, which it takes rare courage even to wish to strip off. No doubt cowardice here, as elsewhere, is folly: for however tragic or desolating the truth may be, it will not be abolished by concealing it, and the facts will operate against us all the more fatally if we childishly insist on not admitting them. Meantime we shall have condemned ourselves to insecurity, confusion, and living with a bad conscience; and we shall have missed the knowledge to which our intellect is by nature addressed: a knowledge that, far from adding to the evils it may discover, masters these evils intellectually and partly balances them by the human and proud pleasure of understanding them.

Nevertheless, the keen air of truth is not for all lungs. The psyche vegetates before she thinks, and when she thinks, far from suspending her vegetative functions, she is merely extending and refining them into a far-reaching sensibility to external influences and probable events. This difficult adjustment has

Loyalty to the truth is wise but difficult.

its excitements and rewards; it fills the spirit with images and passions; yet it is a nuisance to the slumbering organism. There would be more comfort in continuing to pulsate in perfect darkness and freedom. It might be more dangerous, but it would feel safer. If shooting pains or dull obstructions disturbed sometimes that pre-natal bliss, they would serve to heighten the love of it and turn it into a positive ideal. And in fact this ideal remains the background and substance of all our later dreams of Elysium and a Golden Age, of Paradise and Nirvana. In contrast with this, intelligence and the facts discovered by intelligence belong to a world of care, of slavery to external things. The truth, for the psyche, remains always an imposition. Sometimes she bows to it sullenly, sometimes she rebels against it, and angrily maintains that her radical feelings are much more to be trusted. In her happiest moments she forgets the quarrel, and builds, with all the materials that experience has given her, a world of her own not too false to live with for a while, and not so true as to check her animal joy in living. She is an artist, and her world must have the truth and the falsity of art.

This art is not all music or verbal fiction: it is also laborious construction in the realm of matter, or in morality and legislation, imposing on the plastic parts of the world a method agreeable to human interests. Heroic men are intent on reality, but less in reverence for what reality may be, or for the truth of it, than in prophecy of what it ought to be, or may speedily be turned into by their agency. The extreme of energy curiously reverts, in respect to truth, to the extreme of primitive somnolence and vegetative egoism. Edens and millenniums reappear, not now as lost but as future. They are defined and demanded by the native force of the psyche; and such premonitions may be

Inspiration that will not conform to the truth must supersede it.

true if the psyche has the means to realize her purposes
in action. She will then seem to have not only divined
the truth of the future, but miraculously recreated the
world in her own image. Such an apparent miracle
is physically possible and normal, because the psyche
is herself a current in the realm of matter, capable like
any other current of cutting a channel for itself between
banks that will afterwards seem to have come into
being expressly to guide it on its intended course.
Yet just those windings were never prefigured by the
waters at the spring. Either the prophet, then, will
surreptitiously take hints from his worldly wisdom,
or he will be compelled to transpose his prophecy into
a mere ideal, to be realized, if at all, only in another
world, or only within us, that is, only by being stead-
fastly maintained as an ideal in contrast to the
unfortunate truth.

When a man frames a Utopia, and calls it by that
name, he frankly avows the rebellion of his inner man
against the concrete truth; yet if the roots Truth sought
of that vision are very deep in his soul, or in the wrong
if the vision is contagious and people confirm place.
one another in entertaining it, it will not long be called
a Utopia but soon a higher truth, revealed miraculously
and accredited by supernatural faith. To extend the
word truth to such a region puts a great strain on
language and on honesty. A sad waste of spiritual
passion comes of looking for truth where, by the
nature of things, truth is not to be found: in images,
in metaphors, in religion, in moral emotion. These
things, excellent or inevitable in their own sphere,
are rendered inordinate by that pretension: instead of
being poetically beautiful and just, they become
scientifically false and morally fanatical. A better
language would have invented a word other than truth
to express the magic of these visitations. The Greeks
hardly asked whether their religion was true, or how

far their legends about antiquity might be historical.
That would have been a blind and pedantic question.
They asked only that their religion should be traditional
and legal, propitious to the spirit of the city and to the
purgation of private crimes: which myth and worship
might well be, without the mechanism of such bene-
ficence being in the least understood. Myths were
not true and were not false: they were tales appropriate
to tell and to marvel at on specific occasions. They
dramatized the true relations of man to nature, recon-
ciling him to the truth without picturing the truth;
and by their medicinal influence they rendered his
ignorance happy, in the assurance that the truth, if
not always friendly to the grosser man, might be
liberating in the end to the spirit.

The truth is the chosen object, and therefore the
good, of the intellect: of so much of our nature as
demands enlightenment and is concerned
with circumstances or with the past and
future course of existence. But these are
not our only interests, and the truth is
neither our primary good, nor our ultimate good, nor
the synthesis of all goods. By its inclemency, the
truth often drives us indoors, to our home comforts
and familiar affections; and by its precision and contingency—for many things are not true—it also carries
us willingly or unwillingly beyond the truth, into the
region of the imagined or the desired or the beautiful.
Genius is requisite to divine the truth, but not all
kinds of genius take that direction; and a steady affinity
to truth, the whole truth, and nothing but the truth,
while eminently virtuous and honourable, marks rather
a prosaic mind, a cold mind, a mind limited to the safe
middle ground of competence and sagacity. Happiness in the truth is like happiness in marriage, fruitful,
lasting, and ironical. You could not have chosen
better, yet this is not what you dreamt of.

Of spiritual goods it is the most external.

Enthusiasts are consequently seldom satisfied with the truth; they posit something else, much better, warmer, and vaguer. Yet it would chill their enthusiasm to posit this nobler thing as not true, as merely possible or frankly impossible. They have far too dazzling an idea of the truth to recognize the plain truth *That which mystics call truth is something beyond truth.* when they see it: they keep that sacred name for the good, for the all-satisfying, for the ineffable. The consequence is that we have in religion and in idealistic philosophy a baffling reversal of terms: the existent is called appearance, illusion, or privation, whilst something imaginary or notional, or perhaps absolutely blank, is called both reality and truth. That this mystical ultimate good is something in which life issues, or may issue; that it is immediately experienced in moments of ecstasy; that it seems, when found, the sudden solution and quietus for every trouble; all this may be freely admitted by a sober critic; and he will have no serious difficulty in making room for these experiences in his picture of the truth, which should be a description of all existence. Love has a rhetorical habit of heaping all eulogistic terms on one object, no matter how incompatible these terms may be; and in impassioned speculation it is impossible for the most irresponsible intuitions, coming in a trance, not to claim to be called true, although they may annul rather than describe the detail of the world. In reality, the mystic is passing beyond truth. Truth oppresses him, and something beneath or above truth satisfies him completely. He is free to choose; yet however much he may congratulate himself on his flight from existence and from the truth that describes existence, the most that he could legitimately say about his new condition would be that it revealed to him a further region of truth and existence, far superior in his estimation to the region he had abandoned.

The very fact of his salvation would continue to posit the reality of those sins or illusions from which he had been saved: and the truth recognized by him would not be, as he may assert thoughtlessly, *only* his final beatific vision, but this following upon and substituted for his previous experience. If having attained what he calls the truth he shut his eyes to the existence of his previous errors, he would now be hugging the most egregious and egotistical error of all. Not only would he be insisting that a form of being was "true" which perhaps was merely intense and described nothing, but he would be positively denying that this form of being and its relation to all other describable things might be described truly.

Perhaps the fault here touches diction and manners rather than insight.   There is insight in saying that existence is privation, since any fact, in being such as it is, prevents itself, and the truth about it, from being all that is different.   But only a perverse temper would express this by saying that privation was nothing, and that consequently neither suffering, error, nor finitude could at all exist. We might rather say (though this too is hyperbole) that only privation and finitude, involving suffering and error, made existence possible. But finitude does not involve error, if we assert no more than we know; and privation is not suffering if we are willing to be ourselves.

A less mystical religious way of going beyond truth is to personify it.   The truth is not a person: it is not a mind; yet for other reasons we may have conceived a vigilant lawgiver and judge, who will ultimately punish our hidden sins or vindicate our innocence: and evidently such a deity must see in secret, and must be omniscient.   The truth, in all its detail, scope, and eternity, will then lie open to this divine mind: and if we forget for the moment the other attributes of God,

The notion of an omniscient mind personifies truth poetically.

such as power and love, we may say that God not
only knows the truth but *is* the truth existing in act.
The trick of identifying, or not yet distinguishing,
intuition and essence, runs through the history of
speculation and breeds a thousand misunderstandings.
In this case it would be easy to show that intelligence,
though it might eventually traverse all truth in every
direction, would in each act of thought be something
temporal, progressive, and selective, since it is the
utterance of a proposition; so that intelligence moves
in another realm of being from truth, intelligence being
alive and truth being dead. To represent the truth
as living, as the light of universal intuition flooding a
divine mind, dramatizes the truth and puts it before
us as something to be achieved and possessed. This
may pass for a compliment to the truth, and may
facilitate an excited love of it. The business of a good
myth is precisely to humanize the realities which it
plays upon and to render them more amiable. Truth
turned into the thought of an omniscient mind is
enormously glorified, at least in human eyes; yet this
living splendour is not its own. Truth proper is
indifferent to being praised or possessed by anybody:
its sublimity is of another kind; and a love stimulated
by the hope of glory is addressed to dreams of human
achievement rather than to a truly divine truth.

The impulse to dramatize the truth is carried
further in romantic philosophy. Even when personified, the truth remains too external, too   Romantic
chilling and ominous, for a solipsistic poet,   impatience
proud of his every mood, and sure only of   of truth
  cannot
his present sensation. An endless comedy   abolish
of vital errors seems to him worthier of a   truth.
living spirit than a sardonic omniscience. The very
notion of truth, though he cannot banish it altogether,
becomes elusive and ghostly. Why should a free and
unconditioned mind posit a truth at all? Or if the

exigencies of acting and thinking compel a man to posit something, why not posit it, why not posit his whole world, as expressly false, like an actor positing the circumstances set down for him in a play? The truth he posits will be a part of his fiction: it will not pledge or contaminate his creative freedom: and he may say in his heart that he has passed beyond truth.

We have already seen that a perfectly happy creature, one free from hindrance and care, might develop a great sensibility without broaching the idea of truth. A Lucifer might convince himself on internal evidence that he was an uncreated spirit, free to invent romantic societies and gay sciences for his endless entertainment. These he would posit beyond truth, that is, as revealing no compulsion and imposing no responsibility. Lucifer might believe in nothing so long as he did nothing. Ideas, when they are mere ideas, leave us as free and as ignorant as if we had never had them. If a spirit could actually exist *in vacuo*, it might harmlessly posit world after world, positing them as false, or as existing merely in idea. Truth would then not be conceived or invoked at all, yet it would not be annulled. It would hover above the dreaming idealist as ironically as ever; since it would be composed of his whole history, past and future, with his successive fictions *ad infinitum*: something surely unknown to him, being entirely different from any of the worlds which, at various moments, he might have (quite truly) posited as false. Had he ever paused to collect his thoughts and review his illusions, he would at that moment have posited his biography not as false but as true: for he would not now conceive himself to be composing an imaginary biography, a novel about himself, but would be convinced that he had really dreamt all those dreams; and if his whole past and whole future could thus be summoned before his conscience, and he saw the whole truth about himself, I am afraid he would *ipso facto* have stopped living, ceased to posit obviously false sciences and imaginary lives, and felt the truth absorb and paralyse his playful spirit.

For mankind, compelled as we are by our animal status to do and to undergo many specific things, the face of truth is more familiar and less be- *Active life* numbing. We are obliged to believe in *reveals* the postulates we make, and we are obliged *relevant* to make them because they are true. Faith *confirms it.* and truth are thus allied for us from the beginning. A postulate relevant to action is relevant to reality; and where it is action that prompts and controls thought, thought cannot be merely romantic or poetical. It will be initially addressed to immediate and urgent facts; and it will follow the true course and relations of these facts with a rough fidelity. Truth is thus a household presence: not the naked truth nor the divine truth, but truth disguised as a domestic and dressed in homespun. Not to recognize such conventional truths in the home orbit would be idiocy, and to contradict them would be madness.

Yet the same natural life that relies on truth, and is sure of it within this range, inevitably transgresses and overloads the truth which it recognizes. *Moral life* From childhood up we are carried beyond *transcends it.* the truth by our passions, by the qualities and perspectives of our senses, by verbal conventions and beliefs, above all by our vehement judgments about good and evil. There is a sense in which all moral life lies beyond truth. Not, of course, that for an external observer, the whole course of our passionate feelings would not fall within the purview of history and be truly describable; but the living spirit, in which this moral life is actualized and enacted, has other interests besides the interest in truth. The modesty of nature calls for a halt in the direction of knowledge, as in all other directions, not only respecting the depth to which we may penetrate the facts, but also respecting the purity and clearness we may claim for our conceptions.

It would be inhuman and fanatical to set up the truth as the only good. The good is the perfection of life for each creature according to its kind; a perfection which man can never reach without knowledge of his immediate circumstances and his own nature. Potentially, spirit has an innate affinity to all truth, and even to all essence; and this, like all other spiritual interests, is disinterestedly addressed to its ideal object, and terminates there. Yet here spirit is lodged in a specific creature, so that the development of these potential interests can be only partial and mutually qualified. Even charity, a disinterested sympathy with spirit in its every predicament, cannot be impartial in all directions and at all removes. Absolutely universal and unbiassed charity would abet contrary impulses and would utterly dissolve the too sympathetic soul. Truth cannot dictate to love. Will and aspiration move entirely beyond the actual, and forbid the human spirit to attune itself to truth only. Nearer things and lovelier things also solicit us. We must turn to them; yet not without a constant speculative reverence for the truth in its divine immensity.

Yet spirit may outrun truth without contradicting it.

INDEX

Agnosticism, 121
America, v
Anselm, Saint, 7, 8
Aristotle, 97, 100, 124
Athens, 75

Beauty, how related to truth, 115–117
Being, only an essence, 8–10
Berkeley, 21
Byzantium, 103

Cæsar, 83, 84
Categorical imperative, 68, 70
Causation, not necessary, 6, 7 ; underlies "chance", 98
Change, synthesized in intuition, 81
Clough, ii
Coherence, not truth, 42, 43, 114
Contingency of truth, 1, 2
Contraries, how united, 23, 24

Descartes, 59
Dialectic, only mental, 4–5
Dogmatism, its natural origin, 28, 50, 77 ; untenable in morals, 75, 76, 105

Eleatics, 8
Emerson, 74
Empedocles, 111
Error, 40, 41, 46, 63
"Eternal truths", ix, 97–99
Eternity of all truth, ix, x, 79–86

Freud, 63
Future, posited by life, 88–90 ; unequivocal, 94 ; contingent, 95

Hegel, 21, 25, 26, 63
Heidegger, M., referred to, 51
Heraclitus, 25
Hesiod, 111
History, not dialectical, 22–26

Horace, ii, 33
Humanism, 104, 124, 125

"I", the synthetic, not lasting or existent, 85, 86
Idea, of God, ambiguous, 10 ; partly truth hypostasized, 136, 137
Ideas, always express their source, 31, 32 ; modify their object, 33, 34 ; treble sense of the word, 41, 42
Indian philosophy, 8

Johnson, Dr., ii

Kant, 68, 70 ; referred to, 2, *note*

Life, its nature, 71, 73, 113
Locke, 3
Logical correctness touches art, not truth, 12, 13
Logics optional, 17–19, 47, 48
Love of truth, x, 40, 102–118
Lucifer, 138
Lucretius, 111

Marx, 63, 96
Mathematics, application empirical, 2, 3 ; not applicable to spirit, 4
Memory, secondary to expectation, 92, 93
Myth, may convey truth, 62, 63, 65, 66

Napoleon, 54
Necessity, logical only, 1, 2 ; in nature only presumptive, 11
"Now", the, its essence and instances, 84, 85

Occam's Razor, 104, 112
Omniscience, truth personified, 136
Ontological proof, 7–10

141

THE END